A CALVIN TREASURY

A CALVIN TREASURY

Selections from Institutes of the Christian Religion

EDITED BY William F. Keesecker

HARPER & BROTHERS
PUBLISHERS · NEW YORK

The text used in this book is taken from *Institutes of the Christian Religion* by John Calvin, edited by John T. McNeill, translated by Ford Lewis Battles (The Library of Christian Classics, Volumes XX, XXI), Philadelphia: The Westminster Press, copyright © MCMLX W. L. Jenkins, and is used by permission of the publisher.

FIRST EDITION

L-L

Library of Congress catalog card number: 62-7292

PREFACE

The Christian Church possesses in *Institutes of the Christian Religion* a treasure of surpassing worth. It is, however, a treasure which must be rediscovered by each generation. This *A Calvin Treasury* seeks to do. The purpose of the book is to present the heart of Calvin's thought on key themes of Christian faith and life. It is hoped that these brief, to-the-point quotations will be useful to ministers in sermon preparation and private study; to teachers and students as an introductory guide and reference handbook; and to the general reader who may find enjoyment and be stimulated to further, more detailed reading in Calvin's works.

A Calvin Treasury is not intended to be a substitute for the *Institutes*. Indeed, there can be no substitute for thorough reading and study of the complete text. Only thus will the full flavor of the work be tasted. It is recognized, however, that the bulkiness of the *Institutes* creates a formidable barrier to those who have scant time for detailed study. A parish minister, for example, may sincerely intend to read the work from cover to cover, yet his resolution often dies when he surveys the task. It is the hope of the compiler that the selected quotations convey the essence of Calvin's thought in the *Institutes,* and it is equally hoped that in the attempt to aid the reader to enjoy as well as understand Calvin no undue violence has been done his system of thought by the selections made.

Acknowledgment is made to the following periodicals for permission to use quotations which previously appeared in published articles: *Presbyterian Life,* March 15, 1960, "John Calvin Speaks Today." *Monday Morning,* March 15, 1960, "The Human Calvin." *Theology Today,* October, 1960, "John Calvin's Mirror." Permission has been granted by Westminster Press to use the new translation of the *Institutes* published in 1960.

I wish to express my gratitude to Mrs. Elizabeth Potter Smith, librarian of the College of Emporia, Emporia, Kansas, who first aroused my interest in Calvin's writings with a gift of the *Institutes.* I am also indebted to Dr. Arthur A. Hays, late professor of church history at McCormick Theological Seminary, for the original suggestion for the book, and to Dr. Joseph Haroutunian, professor of systematic theology at McCormick Theological Seminary, for reading portions of the manuscript and offering helpful suggestions. I am also grateful to the publisher for editorial assistance, and to Mrs. Ralph Fairman, Mrs. Scott Preston, and Mrs. D. E. Forsblom, who typed the manuscript.

W.F.K.

NOTE TO THE READER

The selections from the *Institutes* have been arranged alphabetically by topics. Source lines at the end of each quotation indicate book, chapter, and section number, in that order, in the *Institutes*. An index of subjects, containing topical cross-references, will be found on pages 149–152. An additional reference index, listing book, chapter, and section of the *Institutes* in numerical sequence, is provided on pages 145–148.

A CALVIN TREASURY

ADOPTION

With what confidence would anyone address God as "Father"?
Who would break forth into such rashness as to claim for himself
the honor of a son of God unless we had been adopted as children
of grace in Christ?   III, xx, 36

Therefore, as God regenerates only the elect with incorruptible
seed forever so that the seed of life sown in their hearts may never
perish, thus he firmly seals the gift of his adoption in them that it
may be steady and sure.   III, ii, 11

AFFLICTION

The Lord also has another purpose for afflicting his people: to
test their patience and to instruct them to obedience. Not that they
can manifest any other obedience to him save what he has given
them. But it so pleases him by unmistakable proofs to make manifest and clear the graces which he has conferred upon the saints, that
these may not lie idle, hidden within. Therefore, by bringing into
the open the power and constancy to forbear, with which he has
endowed his servants, he is said to test their patience.   III, viii, 4

Thus humbled, we learn to call upon his power, which alone
makes us stand fast under the weight of afflictions.   III, viii, 2

ALLEGORY

Allegories ought not to go beyond the limits set by the rule of
Scripture, let alone suffice as the foundation for any doctrines.
III, v, 19

ANGELS

But Scripture strongly insists upon teaching us what could most
effectively make for our consolation and the strengthening of our
faith: namely that angels are dispensers and administrators of God's
beneficence toward us. For this reason, Scripture recalls that they
keep vigil for our safety, take upon themselves our defense, direct
our ways, and take care that some harm may not befall us.
I, xiv, 6

It is certain that spirits lack bodily form, and yet Scripture, matching the measure of our comprehension, usefully depicts for us winged angels under the names of cherubim and seraphim, that we may not doubt that they are ever ready to bring help to us with incredible swiftness, should circumstance require it, even as lightning sent forth from heaven flies to us with its usual speed. Whatever besides can be sought of both their number and order, let us hold it among those mysteries whose full revelation is delayed until the Last Day. Therefore let us remember not to probe too curiously or talk too confidently.   I, XIV, 8

ANTICHRIST

Daniel and Paul foretold that Antichrist would sit in the Temple of God. With us, it is the Roman pontiff we make the leader and standard bearer of that wicked and abominable kingdom.

IV, II, 12

APOSTLES' CREED

Thus far I have followed the order of the Apostles' Creed because it sums up in a few words the main points of our redemption, and thus may serve as a tablet for us upon which we see distinctly and point by point the things in Christ that we ought to heed. I call it the Apostles' Creed without concerning myself in the least as to its authorship. With considerable agreement, the old writers certainly attribute it to the apostles, holding it to have been written and published by the apostles in common, or to be a summary of teaching transmitted by their hands and collected in good faith, and thus worthy of that title. I have no doubt that at the very beginning of the church, in the apostolic age, it was received as a public confession by the consent of all—wherever it originated. It seems not to have been privately written by any one person, since as far back as men can remember it was certainly held to be of sacred authority among all the godly. We consider to be beyond controversy the only point that ought to concern us: that the whole history of our faith is summed up in it succinctly and in definite order, and that it contains nothing that is not vouched for by genuine testimonies of Scripture. This being understood, it is pointless to trouble oneself or quarrel with anyone over the author. Unless, perchance, it is not enough for one to have the certain truth of the Holy Spirit, without at the same time knowing either by whose mouth it was spoken or by whose hand it was written.   II, xvi, 18

APPETITES
It may seem absurd to some that all desires by which man is by nature affected are so completely condemned—although they have been bestowed by God himself, the author of nature. To this I reply that we do not condemn those inclinations which God so engraved upon the character of man at his first creation, that they were eradicable only with humanity itself, but only those bold and unbridled impulses which contend against God's control.   III, iii, 12

ARROGANCE
But if the holy prophets had scruples against separating themselves from the church because of many great misdeeds, not of one man or another but of almost all the people, we claim too much for ourselves if we dare withdraw at once from the communion of the church just because the morals of all do not meet our standard or even square with the profession of Christian faith.   IV, i, 18

ASCENSION (see CHRIST, ASCENSION OF)

ATHEISTS
If, indeed, there were some in the past, and today not a few appear, who deny that God exists, yet willy-nilly they from time to time feel an inkling of what they desire not to believe. One reads of no one who burst forth into bolder or more unbridled contempt of deity than Gaius Caligula; yet no one trembled more miserably when any sign of God's wrath manifested itself; thus—albeit unwillingly—he shuddered at the God whom he professedly sought to despise. You may see now and again how this also happens to those like him; how he who is the boldest despiser of God is of all men the most startled at the rustle of a falling leaf.   I, iii, 2

ATONEMENT

The second requirement of our reconciliation with God was this: that man, who by his disobedience had become lost, should by way of remedy counter it with obedience, satisfy God's judgment, and pay the penalties for sin. Accordingly, our Lord came forth as true man and took the person and the name of Adam in order to take Adam's place in obeying the Father, to present our flesh as the price of satisfaction to God's righteous judgment, and, in the same flesh, to pay the penalty that we had deserved. In short, since neither as God alone could he feel death, nor as man alone could he overcome it, he coupled human nature with divine that to atone for sin he might submit the weakness of the one to death; and that, wrestling with death by the power of the other nature, he might win victory for us.   II, xii, 3

Now we must speak briefly concerning the purpose and use of Christ's priestly office: as a pure and stainless Mediator he is by his holiness to reconcile us to God. But God's righteous curse bars our access to him, and God in his capacity as judge is angry toward us. Hence, an expiation must intervene in order that Christ as priest may obtain God's favor for us and appease his wrath. Thus Christ to perform this office had to come forward with a sacrifice. For under the law, also, the priest was forbidden to enter the sanctuary without blood, that believers might know, even though the priest as their advocate stood between them and God, that they could not propitiate God unless their sins were expiated. The apostle discusses this point at length in The Letter to the Hebrews, from the seventh almost to the end of the tenth chapter. To sum up his argument: The priestly office belongs to Christ alone because by the sacrifice of his death he blotted out our own guilt and made satisfaction for our sins. God's solemn oath, of which he "will not repent," warns us what a weighty matter this is: "You are a priest forever after the order of Melchizedek." God undoubtedly willed in these words to ordain the principal point on which, he knew, our whole salvation turns. For, as has been said, we or our prayers have no access to God unless Christ, as our High Priest, having washed away our sins, sanctifies us and obtains for us that grace from which the uncleanness of our transgressions and vices debars us.   II, xv, 6

This is our acquittal: the guilt that held us liable for punishment has been transferred to the head of the Son of God. We must, above all, remember this substitution, lest we tremble and remain anxious throughout life—as if God's righteous vengeance, which the Son of God has taken upon himself, still hung over us.   II, xvi, 5

Therefore, the beginning of love is righteousness, as Paul describes it: "For our sake he made him to be sin who had done no sin, so that in him we might become the righteousness of God." This means: we, who "by nature are sons of wrath" and estranged from him by sin, have, by Christ's sacrifice, acquired free justification in order to appease God.   II, xvii, 2

If the effect of his shedding of blood is that our sins are not imputed to us, it follows that God's judgment was satisfied by that price.   II, xvii, 4

AUTHORITY (see GOVERNMENT, AUTHORITY OF)

BAPTISM

Now baptism was given to us by God for these ends (which I have taught to be common to all sacraments): first, to serve our faith before him; secondly, to serve our confession before men.   IV, xv, 1

BAPTISM, BENEFITS OF

Lastly, our faith receives from baptism the advantage of its sure testimony to us that we are not only engrafted into the death and life of Christ, but so united to Christ himself that we become sharers in all his blessings.   IV, xv, 6

BAPTISM, CIRCUMCISION AND

Paul forestalls this objection when he immediately adds that the Colossians had been buried with Christ through baptism. By this he means that baptism is today for Christians what circumcision was for the ancients, and that therefore circumcision cannot be enjoined upon Christians without injustice to baptism.   IV, xiv, 24

BAPTISM, INFANT

Yet (you say) there is danger lest he who is ill, if he die without baptism, be deprived of the grace of regeneration. Not at all. God declares that he adopts our babies as his own before they are born, when he promises that he will be our God and the God of our descendants after us. Their salvation is embraced in this word. No one will dare be so insolent toward God as to deny that his promise of itself suffices for its effect.   IV, xv, 20

But this principle will easily and immediately settle the controversy: infants are not barred from the Kingdom of Heaven just because they happen to depart the present life before they have been immersed in water. Yet we have already seen that serious injustice is done to God's covenant if we do not assent to it, as if it were weak of itself, since its effect depends neither upon baptism nor upon any additions.   IV, xv, 22

If it is right for infants to be brought to Christ, why not also to be received into baptism, the symbol of our communion and fellowship with Christ? If the Kingdom of Heaven belongs to them, why is the sign denied which, so to speak, opens to them a door into the church, that, adopted into it, they may be enrolled among the heirs of the Kingdom of Heaven? How unjust of us to drive away those whom Christ calls to himself!   IV, xvi, 7

The children receive some benefit from their baptism: being engrafted into the body of the church, they are somewhat more commended to the other members. Then, when they have grown up, they are greatly spurred to an earnest zeal for worshiping God, by whom they were received as children through a solemn symbol of adoption before they were old enough to recognize him as Father.

IV, xvi, 9

Let us accept as incontrovertible that God is so good and generous to his own as to be pleased, for their sake, also to count among his people the children whom they have begotten.   IV, xvi, 15

For when we consider that immediately from birth God takes and acknowledges them as his children, we feel a strong stimulus to instruct them in an earnest fear of God and observance of the law. Accordingly, unless we wish spitefully to obscure God's goodness, let us offer our infants to him, for he gives them a place among those of his family and household, that is, the members of the church.

IV, xvi, 32

BAPTISM, MODE OF

But whether the person being baptized should be wholly immersed, and whether thrice or once, whether he should only be sprinkled with poured water—these details are of no importance, but ought to be optional to churches according to the diversity of countries. Yet the word "baptize" means to immerse, and it is clear that the rite of immersion was observed in the ancient church.

IV, xv, 19

BAPTISM, POWER OF

But we must realize that at whatever time we are baptized, we are once for all washed and purged for our whole life. Therefore, as often as we fall away, we ought to recall the memory of our baptism and fortify our mind with it, that we may always be sure and confident of the forgiveness of sins.   IV, xv, 3

Paul has accordingly attached a consolation for this purpose: "There is . . . no more condemnation for those who are in Christ Jesus." There he teaches that those whom the Lord has once received into grace, engrafts into the communion of his Christ, and adopts into the society of the church through baptism—so long as they persevere in faith in Christ (even though they are besieged by sin and still carry sin about in themselves)—are absolved of guilt and condemnation.   IV, xv, 12

BAPTISM, SALVATION AND

Few realize how much injury the dogma that baptism is necessary for salvation, badly expounded, has entailed. As a consequence, they are less cautious. For, where the opinion has prevailed that all are lost who have not happened to be baptized with water, our condition is worse than that of God's ancient people—as if the grace of God were now more restricted than under the law! IV, xv, 20

BAPTISM, THE LORD'S SUPPER AND

For baptism attests to us that we have been cleansed and washed; the Eucharistic Supper, that we have been redeemed. In water, washing is represented; in blood, satisfaction. IV, xiv, 22

BISHOPS AND PRESBYTERS (see MINISTRY)

BLOOD

Surely, since in every age, even when the law had not yet been published, the Mediator never was promised without blood, we infer that he was appointed by God's eternal plan to purge the uncleanness of men; for shedding of blood is a sign of expiation. II, xii, 4

BREAD

We are bidden to ask our daily bread that we may be content with the measure that our Heavenly Father has deigned to distribute to us, and not get gain by unlawful devices. Meanwhile, we must hold that it is made ours by title of gift; for, as it is said in Moses, neither effort nor toil, nor our hands, acquire anything for us by themselves but by God's blessing. III, xx, 44

BREVITY

To show the godly man how he may be directed to a rightly ordered life, and briefly to set down some universal rule with which to determine his duties—this will be quite enough for me. Perhaps there will be opportunity for declamations, or I may turn over to others the tasks for which I am not so well suited. By nature I love brevity, and perhaps if I wished to speak more amply it would not be successful. But though a more extended form of teaching were highly acceptable, I would nevertheless scarcely care to undertake it. Moreover, the plan of the present work demands that we give a simple outline of doctrine as briefly as possible.   III, vi, 1

CALL (see MINISTRY)

CALLING

Therefore, God designates as his children those whom he has chosen, and appoints himself their Father. Further, by calling, he receives them into his family and unites them to him so that they may together be one. But when the call is coupled with election, in this way Scripture sufficiently suggests that in it nothing but God's free mercy is to be sought. For if we ask whom he calls, and the reason why, he answers: whom he had chosen.   III, xxiv, 1

The statement of Christ "Many are called but few are chosen" is, in this manner, very badly understood. Nothing will be ambiguous if we hold fast to what ought to be clear from the foregoing: that there are two kinds of call. There is the general call, by which God invites all equally to himself through the outward preaching of the word—even those to whom he holds it out as a savor of death, and as the occasion for severer condemnation. The other kind of call is special, which he deigns for the most part to give to the believers alone, while by the inward illumination of his Spirit he causes the preached Word to dwell in their hearts. Yet sometimes he also causes those whom he illumines only for a time to partake of it; then he justly forsakes them on account of their ungratefulness and strikes them with even greater blindness.   III, xxiv, 8

CHANCE

That this difference may better appear, we must know that God's providence, as it is taught in Scripture, is opposed to fortune and fortuitous happenings. Now it has been commonly accepted in all ages, and almost all mortals hold the same opinion today, that all things come about through chance. What we ought to believe concerning providence is by this depraved opinion most certainly not only beclouded, but almost buried. Suppose a man falls among thieves, or wild beasts; is shipwrecked at sea by a sudden gale; is killed by a falling house or tree. Suppose another man wandering through the desert finds help in his straits; having been tossed by the waves, reachers harbor; miraculously escapes death by a finger's breadth. Carnal reason ascribes all such happenings, whether prosperous or adverse, to fortune. But anyone who has been taught by Christ's lips that all the hairs of his head are numbered will look farther afield for a cause, and will consider all events are governed by God's secret plan.   I, xvi, 2

CHARITY

Rather, each man will so consider with himself that in all his greatness he is a debtor to his neighbors, and that he ought in exercising kindness toward them to set no other limit than the end of his resources; these, as widely as they are extended, ought to have their limits set according to the rule of love.   III, vii, 7

All that I have taught about avoiding offenses I mean to be referred to things intermediate and indifferent. For the things necessary to be done must not be omitted for fear of any offense. For as our freedom must be subordinated to love, so in turn ought love itself to abide under purity of faith. Surely, it is fitting here also to take love into consideration, even as far as to the altar; that is, that for our neighbor's sake we may not offend God.   III, xix, 13

CHASTISEMENT

But the children are beaten with rods, not to pay the penalty for their sins to God, but in order thereby to be led to repentance. Accordingly, we understand that these things have to do rather with the future than with the past. . . . Do not put away the scourge if you do not want to be put away from the inheritance. . . . It will be sufficient to have indicated briefly that the sole purpose of God in punishing his church is that the church may be brought low and repent.   III, iv, 33

CHASTITY

If the Lord requires modesty of us, he condemns whatever opposes it. Consequently, if you aspire to obedience, let neither your heart burn with wicked lust within, nor your eyes wantonly run into corrupt desires, nor your body be decked with bawdy ornaments, nor your tongue seduce your mind to like thoughts with filthy words, nor your appetite inflame it with intemperance. For all vices of this sort are like blemishes, which besmirch the purity of chastity.   II, viii, 44

We shall be content with Chrysostom's tribute alone, because, since he was a particular admirer of virginity, he cannot be regarded as more profuse than the others in commendation of marriage. But here are his words: "The first degree of chastity is sincere virginity; the second, faithful marriage. Therefore, the second sort of virginity is the chaste love of matrimony."   IV, xii, 28

CHILDREN

But sons, who are more generously and candidly treated by their fathers, do not hesitate to offer them incomplete and half-done and even defective works, trusting that their obedience and readiness of mind will be accepted by their fathers, even though they have not quite achieved what their fathers intended. Such children ought we to be, firmly trusting that our services will be approved by our most merciful Father, however small, rude, and imperfect these may be.   III, xix, 5

CHRIST, ASCENSION OF

But by his [Christ's] ascension he fulfilled what he had promised: that he would be with us even to the end of the world. As his body

was raised up above all the heavens, so his power and energy were
diffused and spread beyond all the bounds of heaven and earth.

II, xvi, 14

Scripture itself also not only carefully recounts to us the ascension
of Christ, by which he withdrew the presence of his body from our
sight and company, to shake from us all carnal thinking of him, but
also, whenever it recalls him, bids our minds be raised up, and seek
him in heaven, seated at the right hand of the Father.

IV, xvii, 36

CHRIST, BENEFITS OF

But he [Christ] enjoined them to enter into their own consciences, because "the Kingdom of God . . . is righteousness and
peace and joy in the Holy Spirit." This he did to prevent those
otherwise too much inclined to things earthly from indulging in
foolish dreams of pomp. These words briefly teach us what Christ's
Kingdom confers upon us. For since it is not earthly or carnal and
hence subject to corruption, but spiritual, it lifts us up even to
eternal life. Thus it is that we may patiently pass through this life
with its misery, hunger, cold, contempt, reproaches, and other
troubles—content with this one thing: that our King will never
leave us destitute, but will provide for our needs until, our warfare
ended, we are called to triumph. Such is the nature of his rule, that
he shares with us all that he has received from the Father.

II, xv, 4

Bernard's admonition is worth remembering: "The name of
Jesus is not only light but also food; it is also oil, without which
all food of the soul is dry; it is salt, without whose seasoning whatever is set before us is insipid; finally, it is honey in the mouth,
melody in the ear, rejoicing in the heart, and at the same time medicine. Every discourse in which his name is not spoken is without
savor."   II, xvi, 1

Now therefore, since Christ, the Sun of Righteousness, has shone,
while before there was only dim light, we have the perfect radiance
of divine truth, like the wonted brilliance of midday.   IV, viii, 7

What, then, would it profit us to be gathered under the reign of the Heavenly King, unless beyond this earthly life we were certain of enjoying its benefits? For this reason we ought to know that the happiness promised us in Christ does not consist in outward advantages—such as leading a joyous and peaceful life, having rich possessions, being safe from all harm, and abounding with delights such as the flesh commonly longs after. No, our happiness belongs to the heavenly life! In the world the prosperity and well-being of a people depend partly on an abundance of all good things necessary for the eternal salvation of souls and fortifies them with courage to stand unconquerable against all the assaults of spiritual enemies. From this we infer that he rules—inwardly and outwardly—more for our own sake than his. Hence we are furnished, as far as God knows to be expedient for us, with the gifts of the Spirit, which we lack by nature. By these first fruits we may perceive that we are truly joined to God in perfect blessedness. Then, relying upon the power of the same Spirit, let us not doubt that we shall always be victorious over the devil, the world, and every kind of harmful thing.

II, xv, 4

CHRIST, COMING OF

The fact that the blessed gathering of saintly spirits is called "Abraham's bosom" is enough to assure us of being received after this pilgrimage by the common Father of the faithful, that he may share the fruit of his faith with us. Meanwhile, since Scripture everywhere bids us wait in expectation for Christ's coming, and defers until then the crown of glory, let us be content with the limits divinely set for us: namely, that the souls of the pious, having ended the toil of their warfare, enter into blessed rest, where in glad expectation they await the enjoyment of promised glory, and so all things are held in suspense until Christ the Redeemer appear.

III, xxv, 6

CHRIST, DEATH OF

And for modest minds this answer of Augustine will always be enough: "Since the Father delivered up the Son, and Christ, his body, and Judas, his Lord, why in this delivering up is God just and man guilty, unless because in the one thing they have done, the cause of their doing it is not one?"   I, xviii, 4

CHRIST, DIVINITY OF

Suppose he [Osiander] had only said that Christ, in justifying us, by conjunction of essence becomes ours, not only in that in so far as he is man is he our Head, but also in that the essence of the divine nature is poured into us. Then he would have fed on these delights with less harm, and perhaps such a great quarrel on account of this delusion would not have had to arise. But inasmuch as this principle is like the cuttlefish, which by voiding its black and turbid blood hides its many tails, unless we would knowingly and willingly allow that righteousness to be snatched from us which alone gives us the confidence to glory in our salvation, we must bitterly resist.   III, xi, 6

CHRIST, INCARNATION OF

Here is something marvelous: the Son of God descended from heaven in such a way that, without leaving heaven, he willed to be borne in the virgin's womb, to go about the earth, and to hang upon the cross; yet he continuously filled the world even as he had done from the beginning!   II, xiii, 4

CHRIST, INDWELLING

We must now examine this question. How do we receive those benefits which the Father bestowed on his only-begotten Son—not for Christ's own private use, but that he might enrich poor and needy men? First, we must understand that as long as Christ remains outside of us, and we are separated from him, all that he has suffered and done for the salvation of the human race remains useless and of no value for us. Therefore, to share with us what he has received from the Father, he had to become ours and to dwell within us.   III, i, 1

CHRIST, MEDIATOR (see MEDIATOR)

CHRIST, VIRGIN BIRTH OF

Therefore, it is readily inferred from Matthew's words that because Christ was begotten of Mary, he was engendered from her seed, just as when Boaz is said to have been begotten of Rahab a similar generation is meant. And Matthew does not here describe the virgin as a channel through which Christ flowed. Rather, he differentiates this wonderful manner of generation from the common sort in stating that through her Christ was begotten of the seed of David. In the same way that Isaac was begotten of Abraham, Solomon of David, Joseph of Jacob, Christ is said to have been begotten of his mother. For the Evangelist so arranges the order of his words. Meaning to prove that Christ took his origin from David, he was satisfied with this one thing: Christ was begotten of Mary. From this it follows that he took it as generally acknowledged that Mary was related to Joseph.   II, xiii, 3

CHRISTIAN LIFE, THE

Now the great thing is this: we are consecrated and dedicated to God in order that we may thereafter think, speak, meditate, and do, nothing except to his glory. For a sacred thing may not be applied to profane uses without marked injury to him.

If we, then, are not our own but the Lord's, it is clear what error we must flee, and whither we must direct all the acts of our life.

We are not our own: let not our reason nor our will, therefore, sway our plans and deeds. We are not our own: let us therefore not set it as our goal to seek what is expedient for us according to the flesh. We are not our own: in so far as we can, let us therefore forget ourselves and all that is ours.

Conversely, we are God's: let us therefore live for him and die for him. We are God's: let his wisdom and will therefore rule all our actions. We are God's: let all the parts of our life accordingly strive toward him as our only lawful goal. O, how much has that man profited who, having been taught that he is not his own, has taken away dominion and rule from his own reason that he may yield it to God! For, as consulting our self-interest is the pestilence that most effectively leads to our destruction, so the sole haven of salvation is to be wise in nothing and to will nothing through ourselves but to follow the leading of the Lord alone.   III, vii, 1

CHRISTIAN LIFE, CONSISTENCY OF THE

Accordingly, the Christian must surely be so disposed and minded that he feels within himself it is with God he has to deal throughout his life.   III, vii, 2

CHRISTIANS

The believers stand unconquered through the strength of their king, and his spiritual riches abound in them. Hence they are justly called Christians.   II, xv, 5

CHURCH, CATHOLIC

The church is called "catholic," or "universal," because there could not be two or three churches unless Christ be torn asunder— which cannot happen!   IV, i, 2

CHURCH, COMPOSITION OF THE

For we have said that Holy Scripture speaks of the church in two ways. Sometimes by the term "church" it means that which is actually in God's presence, into which no persons are received but those who are children of God by grace of adoption and true members of Christ by sanctification of the Holy Spirit. Then, indeed, the church includes not only the saints presently living on earth, but all the elect from the beginning of the world. Often, however, the name "church" designates the whole multitude of men spread over the earth who profess to worship one God and Christ. By baptism we are initiated into faith in him; by partaking in the Lord's Supper

we attest our unity in true doctrine and love; in the Word of the
Lord we have agreement, and for the preaching of the Word the
ministry instituted by Christ is preserved.   IV, 1, 7

CHURCH, DIFFERENCES IN THE

But I say we must not thoughtlessly forsake the church because of
any petty dissensions. For in it alone is kept safe and uncorrupted
that doctrine in which piety stands sound and the use of the sacraments ordained by the Lord is guarded.   IV, 1, 12

CHURCH, TRUE

From this the face of the church comes forth and becomes visible
to our eyes. Wherever we see the Word of God purely preached and
heard, and the sacraments administered according to Christ's institution, there, it is not to be doubted, a church of God exists. For
his promise cannot fail: "Wherever two or three are gathered in my
name, there I am in the midst of them."   IV, 1, 9

CONFESSION, ABSOLUTION AND

Therefore, it follows that certainty of binding and loosing does
not lie within the competence of earthly judgment because the
minister of the word, when he duly performs his functions, can
absolve only conditionally. But this is said for the sake of sinners,
"If you forgive the sins of any," etc., lest they should doubt whether
the pardon promised in God's commandment and Word will be
ratified in heaven.   III, IV, 18

CONFESSION, FORMAL

And indeed, we see this custom observed with good result in well-
regulated churches: that every Lord's Day the minister frames the
formula of confession in his own and the people's name, and by it
he accuses all of wickedness and implores pardon from the Lord.
In short, with this key a gate to prayer is opened both to individuals
in private and to all in public.   III, IV, 11

Scripture, moreover, approves two forms of private confession: one made for our own sake, to which the statement of James refers that we should confess our sins to one another. For he means that, disclosing our weaknesses to one another, we help one another with mutual counsel and consolation. The other form we are to use for our neighbor's sake, to appease him and to reconcile him to us if through fault of ours he has been in any way injured.   III, IV, 12

CONFESSION, TO PRIESTS

If we must confess to priestlings alone, then we must pray for them alone.   III, IV, 6

If you are embarrassed to tell anyone what sins you have committed, recite them daily to your own soul. I do not tell you to confess them to your fellow servant, who may upbraid you. Recite them to God who heals them.   III, IV, 8

CONFESSION, VOLUNTARY

Therefore, let every believer remember that, if he be privately troubled and afflicted with a sense of sins, so that without outside help he is unable to free himself from them, it is a part of his duty not to neglect what the Lord has offered to him by way of remedy. Namely, that, for his relief, he should use private confession to his own pastor; and for his solace, he should beg the private help of him whose duty it is, both publicly and privately, to comfort the people of God by the gospel teaching. But he should always observe this rule: that where God prescribes nothing definite, consciences be not bound with a definite yoke. Hence, it follows that confession of this sort ought to be free so as not to be required of all, but to be commended only to those who know that they have need of it.
     III, IV, 12

CONFIRMATION

How I wish that we might have kept the custom which, as I have said, existed among the ancient Christians before this misborn wraith of a sacrament came to birth! Not that it would be a confirmation such as they fancy, which cannot be named without doing injustice to baptism; but a catechizing, in which children or those near adolescence would give an account of their faith before the church. . . . If this discipline were in effect today, it would certainly arouse some slothful parents, who carelessly neglect the instruction of their children as a matter of no concern to them; for them they could not overlook it without public disgrace. There would be greater agreement in faith among Christian people, and not so many would go untaught and ignorant; some would not be so rashly carried away with new and strange doctrines; in short, all would have some methodical instruction, so to speak, in Christian doctrine.   IV, xix, 13

CONSCIENCE, GUILTY

But it is especially our conscience itself that, weighed down by a mass of sins, now complains and groans, now accuses itself, now murmurs secretly, now breaks out in open tumult. And so, whether adversities reveal God's wrath, or the conscience finds in itself the proof and ground thereof, thence unbelief obtains weapons and devices to overthrow faith. Yet these are always directed to this objective: that, thinking God to be against us and hostile to us, we should not hope for any help from him, and should fear him as if he were our deadly enemy. To bear these attacks faith arms and fortifies itself with the Word of the Lord.   III, ii, 20–21

CONSCIENCE, NATURE OF

To resolve this difficulty it first behooves us to comprehend what conscience is: we must seek the definition from the derivation of the word. For just as when through the mind and understanding men grasp a knowledge of things, and from this are said "to know," this is the source of the word "knowledge," so also when they have a sense of divine judgment, as a witness joined to them, which does not allow them to hide their sins from being accused before the Judge's tribunal, this sense is called "conscience." For it is a certain mean between God and man, because it does not allow man to suppress within himself what he knows, but pursues him to the point of convicting him.   III, xix, 15

Therefore, as works have regard to men, so conscience refers to God. A good conscience, then, is nothing but inward integrity of heart.   III, xix, 16

CONSCIENCE, OTHERS AND

Hence it happens that the law is said to bind the conscience when it simply binds man, without regard to other men, or without having any consideration for them. For example: God not only teaches us to keep our mind chaste and pure from all lust, but forbids any obscenity of speech and outward wantonness. My conscience is subject to the observance of this law, even though no man were alive in the world. Thus, he who conducts himself intemperately sins not so much because he furnishes a bad example to his brethren as in that his conscience is bound with guilt before God.   IV, x, 4

CONSCIENCE, WORK OF

For our conscience does not allow us to sleep a perpetual insensible sleep without being an inner witness and monitor of what we owe God, without holding before us the difference between good and evil and thus accusing us when we fail in our duty.   II, viii, 1

CONTROVERSY

Now, for my part, when there is a dispute concerning anything, I am stupid enough to refer everything back to the definition itself, which is the hinge and foundation of the whole debate.   III, iv, 1

CONVERSION

If in a stone there is such plasticity that, made softer by some means, it becomes somewhat bent, I will not deny that man's heart can be molded to obey the right, provided what is imperfect in him be supplied by God's grace. But if by this comparison the Lord wished to show that nothing good can ever be wrung from our heart, unless it become wholly other, let us not divide between him and us what he claims for himself alone. If, therefore, a stone is transformed into flesh when God converts us to zeal for the right, whatever is of our own will is effaced. What takes its place is wholly from God. I say that the will is effaced; not in so far as it is will, for in man's conversion what belongs to his primal nature remains entire. I also say that it is created anew; not meaning that the will now begins to exist, but that it is changed from an evil to a good will.

II, iii, 6

Accordingly, we are restored by this regeneration through the benefit of Christ into the righteousness of God; from which we had fallen through Adam. In this way it pleases the Lord fully to restore whomsoever he adopts into the inheritance of life. And indeed, this restoration does not take place in one moment or one day or one year; but through continual and sometimes even slow advances God wipes out in his elect the corruptions of the flesh, cleanses them of guilt, consecrates them to himself as temples renewing all their minds to true purity that they may practice repentance throughout their lives and know that this warfare will end only at death.

III, iii, 9

CORRECTION

Yet that holy man, having a remarkable zeal for edification, tempers his method of teaching the truth so that as far as possible he prudently avoids giving offense. For he reminds us that those things which are truly said can at the same time be fittingly said. If anyone addresses the people in this way: "If you do not believe, the reason is that you have already been divinely destined for destruction," he not only fosters sloth but also gives place to evil intention. If anyone extends to the future also the statement that they who hear will not believe because they have been condemned, this will be cursing rather than teaching. Augustine, therefore, rightly bids such men begone from the church, as foolish teachers or perverse and foreboding prophets. Elsewhere he contends for the opinion that a man benefits by rebuke when he who causes whom he will to profit even without rebuke shows mercy and lends help. But why is it this way with one man, another way with another? Far be it from us to say that judgment belongs to the clay, not to the potter!   III, xxiii, 14

CREATION

But creation is not inpouring, but the beginning of essence out of nothing.   I, xv, 5

CROSS, A REMEDY

Thus, lest in the unmeasured abundance of our riches we go wild; lest, puffed up with honors, we become proud; lest, swollen with other good things—either of the soul or of the body, or of fortune —we grow haughty, the Lord himself, according as he sees it expedient, confronts us and subjects and restrains our unrestrained flesh with the remedy of the cross. And this he does in various ways in accordance with what is healthful for each man.   III, viii, 5

CROSS, BEARING THE

But it behooves the godly mind to climb still higher, to the height to which Christ calls his disciples; that each must bear his own cross. For whomever the Lord has adopted and deemed worthy of his fellowship ought to prepare themselves for a hard, toilsome, and unquiet life, crammed with very many and various kinds of evil. It is the Heavenly Father's will thus to exercise them so as to put his own children to a definite test. Beginning with Christ, his first-born, he follows this plan with all his children.   III, viii, 1

You see that patiently to bear the cross is not to be utterly stupefied and to be deprived of all feeling of pain. It is not as the Stoics of old foolishly described "the great-souled man": one who, having cast off all human qualities, was affected equally by adversity and prosperity, by sad times and happy ones—nay, who like a stone was not affected at all. And what did this sublime wisdom profit them? They painted a likeness of forbearance that has never been found among men, and can never be realized. Rather, while they want to possess a forbearance too exact and precise, they have banished its power from human life. . . . Yet we have nothing to do with this iron philosophy which our Lord and Master has condemned not only by his word, but also by his example.   III, viii, 9

CROSS, PREACHING OF THE

This magnificent theater of heaven and earth, crammed with innumerable miracles, Paul calls the "wisdom of God." Contemplating it, we ought in wisdom to have known God. But because we have profited so little by it, he calls us to the faith of Christ, which, because it appears foolish, the unbelievers despise. Therefore, although the preaching of the cross does not agree with our human inclination, if we desire to return to God our Author and Maker, from whom we have been estranged, in order that he may again begin to be our Father, we ought nevertheless to embrace it humbly.

II, vi, 1

CROSS, RESURRECTION AND THE

To conclude in a word: if believers' eyes are turned to the power of the resurrection, in their hearts the cross of Christ will at last triumph over the devil, flesh, sin, and wicked men.   III, ix, 6

CROSS, WILL OF GOD AND THE

And indeed, unless Christ had been crucified according to God's will, whence would we have redemption?   I, xviii, 3

CURIOSITY

When a certain shameless fellow mockingly asked a pious old man what God had done before the creation of the world, the latter aptly countered that he had been building hell for the curious.

I, xiv, 1

Let no one grumble here that God could have provided better for our salvation if he had forestalled Adam's fall. Pious minds ought to loathe this objection, because it manifests inordinate curiosity. Furthermore, the matter has to do with the secret of predestination, which will be discussed later in its proper place.   II, i, 10

Human curiosity renders the discussion of predestination, already somewhat difficult of itself, very confusing and even dangerous. No restraints can hold it back from wandering in forbidden bypaths and thrusting upward to the heights. If allowed, it will leave no secret to God that it will not search out and unravel.   III, xxi, 1

I desire only to have them generally admit that we should not investigate what the Lord has left hidden in secret, that we should not neglect what he has brought into the open, so that we may not be convicted of excessive curiosity on the one hand, or of excessive ingratitude on the other.   III, xxi, 4

DEATH

Indeed, for those who think only of the present life death is the final despair, but this could not cut off Job's hope. "Even if he slay me," he said, "I shall nonetheless hope in him."   II, x, 19

Surely it is terrifying to walk in the darkness of death; and believers, whatever their strength may be, cannot but be frightened by it. But since the thought prevails that they have God beside them, caring for their safety, fear at once yields to assurance.

III, ii, 21

DEPRAVITY

These examples, accordingly, seem to warn us against adjudging man's nature wholly corrupted, because some men have by its prompting not only excelled in remarkable deeds, but conducted themselves most honorably throughout life.   II, iii, 3

DETERMINATION, CALVIN'S

Last winter when I thought the quartan fever was summoning me to my death, the more the disease pressed upon me the less I spared myself, until I could leave a book behind me that might, in some measure, repay the generous invitation of godly men.

PREFACE

DEVIL, LIMITATION OF THE (see also SATAN)

Therefore God does not allow Satan to rule over the souls of believers, but gives over only the impious and unbelievers, whom he deigns not to regard as members of his own flock, to be governed by him.   I, xiv, 18

DEVIL, REALITY OF THE

Inasmuch as we have before refuted that trifling philosophy about the holy angels which teaches that they are nothing but good inspirations or impulses which God arouses in men's minds, so also in this place ought those men to be refuted who babble of devils as nothing else than evil emotions or perturbations which come upon us from our flesh.   I, xiv, 19

DEVIL, SKILL OF THE

We have been forewarned that an enemy relentlessly threatens us, an enemy who is the very embodiment of rash boldness, of military prowess, of crafty wiles, of untiring zeal and haste, of every conceivable weapon and of skill in the science of warfare. We must, then, bend our every effort to this goal: that we should not let ourselves be overwhelmed by carelessness or faintheartedness, but on the contrary, with courage rekindled stand our ground in combat. Since this military service ends only at death, let us urge ourselves to perseverance.   I, xiv, 13

DEVIL, WICKEDNESS OF THE

Yet, since the devil was created by God, let us remember that this malice, which we attribute to his nature, came not from his creation but from his perversion. For, whatever he has that is to be condemned he has derived from his revolt and fall.   I, xiv, 16

DEVIL, WORK OF THE

As for the discord and strife that we say exists between Satan and God, we ought to accept as a fixed certainty the fact that he can do nothing unless God wills and assents to it . . . and so he obeys his Creator, whether he will or not, because he is compelled to yield him service wherever God impels him.   I, xiv, 17

Now, because God bends the unclean spirits hither and thither at will, he so governs their activity that they exercise believers in combat, ambush them, invade their peace, beset them in combat, and also often weary them, rout them, terrify them, and sometimes wound them; yet they never vanquish or crush them.   I, xiv, 18

DISCIPLINE

Albeit the Lord's Word, which here ought to be our sole rule, surely prescribes a greater moderation. For it teaches that disciplinary rigor is not to be pushed so far that that man for whom it ought to be chiefly concerned becomes overwhelmed with sorrow. This we have discussed more fully above.   IV, i, 29

But because some persons, in their hatred of discipline, recoil from its very name, let them understand this: if no society, indeed, no house which has even a small family, can be kept in proper condition without discipline, it is much more necessary in the church, whose condition should be as ordered as possible.   IV, xii, 1

But we ought not to pass over the fact that such severity as is joined with a "spirit of gentleness" befits the church.   IV, xii, 8

DISOBEDIENCE

Since the woman through unfaithfulness was led away from God's Word by the serpent's deceit, it is already clear that disobedience was the beginning of the Fall. This Paul also confirms, teaching that all were lost through the disobedience of one man.   II, i, 4

DOCTRINE

For not all the articles of true doctrine are of the same sort. Some are so necessary to know that they should be certain and unquestioned by all men as the proper principles of religion. Such are: God is one; Christ is God and the Son of God; our salvation rests in

God's mercy; and the like. Among the churches there are other
articles of doctrine disputed which still do not break the unity of
faith. Suppose that one church believes—short of unbridled contention and opinionated stubbornness—that souls upon leaving bodies
, fly to heaven; while another, not daring to define the place, is convinced nevertheless that they live to the Lord. What churches would
disagree on this one point? Here are the apostle's words: "Let us
therefore, as many as are perfect, be of the same mind; and if you
be differently minded in anything, God shall reveal this also to
you."   IV, i, 12

We therefore teach that faithful ministers are now not permitted
to coin any new doctrine, but that they are simply to cleave to that
doctrine to which God has subjected all men without exception.

IV, viii, 9

Indeed, what is the beginning of true doctrine but a prompt
eagerness to hearken to God's voice?   I, vii, 5

EATING

The rule of quantity in this is that we should eat more sparingly
and lightly than is our custom; only for need, not also for pleasure.

IV, xii, 18

ELECT, THE

Why, then, according to the apostle, are believers crowned. Because they have been chosen and called and justified by the Lord's
mercy, not by their own effort.   II, v, 2

If anyone wants a clearer answer, here it is: God works in his
elect in two ways: within, through his Spirit; without, through his
Word. By his Spirit, illuminating their minds and forming their
hearts to the love and cultivation of righteousness, he makes them a
new creation. By his Word, he arouses them to desire, to seek after,
and to attain that same renewal.   II, v, 5

For here we are not bidden to distinguish between reprobate and elect—that is for God alone, not for us, to do—but to establish with certainty in our hearts that all those who, by the kindness of God the Father, through the working of the Holy Spirit, have entered into fellowship with Christ, are set apart as God's property and personal possession; and that when we are of their number we share that great grace.   IV, I, 3

ELECTION, A UNIVERSAL POSSIBILITY
If all men in general bowed the knee before Christ, election would be general; now in the fewness of believers a manifest diversity appears.   III, XXII, 7

ELECTION, CERTAINTY OF
Although it is now sufficiently clear that God by his secret plan freely chooses whom he pleases, rejecting others, still his free election has been only half explained until we come to individual persons, to whom God not only offers salvation but so assigns it that the certainty of its effect is not in suspense or doubt.   III, XXI, 7

ELECTION, END OF
Yet Paul teaches that we have been chosen to this end: that we may lead a holy and blameless life. If election has as its goal holiness of life, it ought rather to arouse and goad us eagerly to set our mind upon it than to serve as a pretext for doing nothing. What a great difference there is between these two things: to cease well-doing because election is sufficient for salvation, and to devote ourselves to the pursuit of good as the appointed goal of election! Away, then, with such sacrileges, for they wickedly invert the whole order of election. But they stretch their blasphemies farther when they say that he who has been condemned by God, if he endeavors through innocent and upright life to make himself approved of God, will lose his labor. In this contention they are convicted of utterly shameless falsehood. Whence could such endeavor arise but from election? For whoever are of the number of the reprobate, as they are vessels made for dishonor, so they do not cease by their

continual crimes to arouse God's wrath against themselves, and to
confirm by clear signs that God's judgment has already been pro-
nounced upon them—no matter how much they vainly resist it.

III, xxiii, 12

ELECTION, FAULTY

Yet it daily happens that those who seemed to be Christ's, fall
away from him again, and hasten to destruction. Indeed, in that
same passage, where he declares that none of those whom the Father
had given to him perished, he nevertheless, excepts the son of perdi-
tion. True indeed, but it is also equally plain that such persons
never cleaved to Christ with the heartfelt trust in which certainty
of election has, I say, been established for us.   III, xxiv, 7

ELECTION, SIGNS OF

Therefore, as it is wrong to make the force of election contingent
upon faith in the gospel, by which we feel that it appertains to us,
so we shall be following the best order if, in seeking the certainty of
our election, we cling to those latter signs which are sure attesta-
tions of it. Satan has no more grievous or dangerous temptation
to dishearten believers than when he unsettles them with doubt
about their election, while at the same time he arouses them with a
wicked desire to seek it outside the way. I call it "seeking outside
the way" when mere man attempts to break into the inner recesses
of divine wisdom, and tries to penetrate even to highest eternity, in
order to find out what decision has been made concerning himself at
God's judgment seat.   III, xxiv, 4

First, if we seek God's fatherly mercy and kindly heart, we should
turn our eyes to Christ, on whom alone God's Spirit rests.

III, xxiv, 5

The fact that, as we said, the firmness of our election is joined to
our calling is another means of establishing our assurance. For
those whom Christ has illumined with the knowledge of his name
and has introduced into the bosom of his church, he is said to receive into his care and keeping.   III, xxiv, 6

ELECTION, SOURCE OF

Surely there is ready and sufficient reason to believe that good takes its origin from God alone. And only in the elect does one find a will inclined to good. Yet we must seek the cause of election outside men. It follows, thence, that man has a right will not from himself, but that it flows from the same good pleasure by which we were chosen before the creation of the world.   II, III, 8

ELECTION, WILL AND

Now we must examine the will, upon which freedom of decision especially depends; for we have already seen that choice belongs to the sphere of the will rather than to that of the understanding.

II, II, 26

EQUITY

What I have said will become plain if in all laws we examine, as we should, these two things: the constitution of the law, and the equity on which its constitution is itself founded and rests. Equity, because it is natural, cannot but be the same for all, and therefore, this same purpose ought to apply to all laws, whatever their object. . . . Hence, this equity alone must be the goal and rule and limit of all laws.   IV, xx, 16

ERROR

Almost all errors have commonly taken their occasion from truth.

II, VII, 14

EVIL

And whence, I ask you, comes the stench of a corpse, which is both putrefied and laid open by the heat of the sun? All men see that it is stirred up by the sun's rays; yet no one for this reason says that the rays stink. Thus, since the matter and guilt of evil repose in a wicked man, what reason is there to think that God contracts any defilement, if he uses his service for his own purpose? Away, therefore, with this dog-like impudence, which can indeed bark at God's justice afar off but cannot touch it.   I, xvii, 5

God so uses the works of the ungodly, and so bends their minds to carry out his judgments, that he remains pure from every stain.

I, xviii, 1

We ought, indeed, to hold fast by this: while God accomplishes through the wicked what he has decreed by his secret judgment, they are not excusable, as if they had obeyed his precept which out of their own lust they deliberately break.   I, xviii, 4

EXCOMMUNICATION

In such corrections and excommunication, the church has three ends in view. The first is that they who lead a filthy and infamous life may not be called Christians, to the dishonor of God, as if his holy church were a conspiracy of wicked and abandoned men.

The second purpose is that the good be not corrupted by the constant company of the wicked, as commonly happens.

The third purpose is that those overcome by shame for their baseness begin to repent.   IV, xii, 5

FAITH, ASSURANCE OF

For faith does not certainly promise itself either length of years or honor or riches in this life, since the Lord willed that none of these things be appointed for us. But it is content with this certainty: that, however many things fail us that have to do with the maintenance of this life, God will never fail. Rather, the chief assurance of faith rests in the expectation of the life to come, which has been placed beyond doubt through the Word of God.

III, ii, 28

We make the freely given promise of God the foundation of faith because upon it faith properly rests.   III, ii, 29

FAITH, DEFINITION OF

Now we shall possess a right definition of faith if we call it a firm and certain knowledge of God's benevolence toward us, founded upon the truth of the freely given promise in Christ, both revealed to our minds and sealed upon our hearts through the Holy Spirit.   III, ii, 7

FAITH, HOPE AND

Thus, faith believes God to be true, hope awaits the time when his truth shall be manifested; faith believes that he is our Father, hope anticipates that he will ever show himself to be a Father toward us; faith believes that eternal life has been given to us, hope anticipates that it will some time be revealed; faith is the foundation upon which hope rests, hope nourishes and sustains faith.

III, ii, 42

Because of this connection and kinship, Scriptures sometimes uses the words "faith" and "hope" interchangeably.   III, ii, 43

FAITH, IN GOD

For unbelief is so deeply rooted in our hearts, and we are so inclined to it, that not without hard struggle is each one able to persuade himself of what all confess with the mouth: namely, that God is faithful.   III, ii, 15

FAITH, LOVE AND

By faith, therefore, we gain forgiveness; by love we give thanks and testify to the Lord's kindness.   III, iv, 37

FAITH, PURPOSE OF

Even though the apostle assigns to believers alone the honor of being one with Christ, it does not follow that unbelievers cannot be born of the same source. For example, when we say that Christ was made man that he might make us children of God, this expression does not extend to all men. For faith intervenes, to engraft us spiritually into the body of Christ.   II, xiii, 2

FAITH, SUBSTANCE OF

Is this what believing means—to understand nothing, provided only that you submit your feeling obediently to the church? Faith rests not on ignorance, but on knowledge. And this is, indeed, knowledge not only of God but of the divine will.   III, ii, 2

But on this pretext it would be the height of absurdity to label ignorance tempered by humility "faith"! For faith consists in the knowledge of God and Christ, not in reverence for the church.

III, ii, 3

FAITH, TRIALS OF

Yet I do not deny what I stated above: that certain interruptions of faith occasionally occur, according as its weakness is violently buffeted hither and thither; so in the thick darkness of temptations its light is snuffed out. Yet whatever happens, it ceases not its earnest quest for God.   III, ii, 24

FAITH, WORD AND

In understanding faith it is not merely a question of knowing that God exists, but also—and this especially—of knowing what is his will toward us. For it is not so much our concern to know who he is in himself, as what he wills to be toward us. Now, therefore, we hold faith to be a knowledge of God's will toward us, perceived from his Word.

First, we must be reminded that there is a permanent relationship between faith and the Word. He could not separate one from the other any more than we could separate the rays from the sun from which they come.   III, ii, 6

FASTING, END OF

Holy and lawful fasting has three objectives. We use it either to weaken and subdue the flesh that it may not act wantonly, or that we may be better prepared for prayers and holy meditations, or that it may be a testimony of our self-abasement before God when we wish to confess our guilt before him.   IV, xii, 15

FASTING, METHOD IN

In like manner, the pastors of the church would not be doing ill today if, when they see ruin hanging over the necks of their people, they were to cry out to them to hasten to fasting and weeping; provided—and this is the principal point—they always urge with greater and more intent care and effort that "they should rend their hearts and not their garments."   III, iii, 17

FATE

Even though we are unwilling to quarrel over words, yet we do not admit the word "fate," both because it is one of those words whose profane novelties Paul teaches us to avoid, and because men try by the odium it incurs to oppress God's truth. Indeed, we are falsely and maliciously charged with this very dogma. We do not, with the Stoics, contrive a necessity out of the perpetual connection and intimately related series of causes, which is contained in nature; but we make God the ruler and governor of all things, who in accordance with his wisdom has from the farthest limit of eternity decreed what he was going to do, and now by his might carries out what he has decreed. From this we declare that not only heaven and earth and the inanimate creatures, but also the plans and intentions of men, are so governed by his providence that they are borne by it straight to their appointed end.   I, xvi, 8

FATHERS

Thus, in him who is our father we should recognize something divine because he does not bear the divine title without cause.

II, viii, 35

It makes no difference whether our superiors are worthy or unworthy of this honor, for whatever they are they have attained their position through God's providence—a proof that the Lawgiver himself would have us hold them in honor.   II, viii, 36

FAULTS

We delight in a certain poisoned sweetness experienced in ferreting out and in disclosing the evils of others.   II, viii, 48

FEAR

And all the Israelites together, whenever they arm themselves by remembering the covenant, sufficiently assert that since God so enjoins, one is not to pray fearfully. In this they followed the examples of the patriarchs, especially Jacob, who, after he confessed himself to be less than the many mercies he had received at God's hand, says that he is nevertheless encouraged to ask greater things because God had promised that he would do them.   III, xx, 14

FLATTERY

There is, indeed, nothing that man's nature seeks more eagerly than to be flattered. Accordingly, when his nature becomes aware that its gifts are highly esteemed, it tends to be unduly credulous about them. It is thus no wonder that the majority of men have erred so perniciously in this respect. For since blind self-love is innate in all mortals, they are most freely persuaded that nothing inheres in themselves that deserves to be considered hateful. Thus even with no outside support the utterly vain opinion generally obtains credence that man is abundantly sufficient of himself to lead a good and blessed life.   II, i, 2

FOOD

Surely we experience this: with a full stomach our mind is not so lifted up to God that it can be drawn to prayer with a serious and ardent affection and persevere in it.   IV, xii, 16

FORGIVENESS

So carrying, as we do, the traces of sin around with us throughout life, unless we are sustained by the Lord's constant grace in forgiving our sins, we shall scarcely abide one moment in the church.
                                                                    IV, i, 21

FREE WILL

Few have defined what free will is, although it repeatedly occurs in the writings of all. Origen seems to have put forward a definition generally agreed upon among ecclesiastical writers when he said that it is a faculty of the reason to distinguish between good and evil, a faculty of the will to choose one or the other. Augustine does not disagree with this when he teaches that it is a faculty of the reason and the will to choose good with the assistance of grace; evil, when grace is absent.   II, ii, 4

If this be admitted, it will be indisputable that free will is not sufficient to enable man to do good works, unless he be helped by grace, indeed by special grace, which only the elect receive through regeneration.   II, ii, 6

Let others trust as they will in their own capacities and powers of free choice, which they seem to themselves to possess. For us let it be enough that we stand and are strong in God's power alone.

III, xx, 46

GOD, ANGER OF

From the other side we see that God, while not ceasing to love his children, is wondrously angry toward them; not because he is disposed of himself to hate them, but because he would frighten them by the feeling of his wrath in order to humble their fleshly pride, shake off their sluggishness, and arouse them to repentance. Therefore, at the same time they conceive him to be at once angry and merciful toward them, or toward their sins. For they unfeignedly pray that his wrath be averted, while with tranquil confidence they nevertheless flee to him for refuge.   III, ii, 12

GOD, ARTISTRY OF

The first part of the rule is exemplified when we reflect upon the greatness of the Artificer who stationed, arranged, and fitted together the starry host of heaven in such wonderful order that nothing more beautiful in appearance can be imagined; who so set and fixed some in their stations that they cannot move; who granted to

others a freer course, but so as not to wander outside their appointed course; who so adjusted the motion of all that days and
nights, months, years, and seasons of the year are measured off; who
so proportioned the inequality of days, which we daily observe, that
no confusion occurs. It is so too when we observe his power in sus-
taining so great a mass, in governing the swiftly revolving heavenly
system, and the like. For these few examples make sufficiently clear
what it is to recognize God's powers in the creation of the universe.

I, xiv, 21

GOD, AVERSION TO

Surely, as we are naturally turned away from God, unless self-
denial precedes, we shall never approach that which is right.

III, iii, 8

GOD, CHARACTER OF

What is God? Men who pose this question are merely toying with
idle speculations. It is far better for us to inquire, "What is his nature?" and to know what is consistent with his nature.   I, ii, 2

GOD, DECREES OF

But let us not doubt that God has done everything wisely and
justly—as all godly persons ought to believe—even if we often do not
know the reason why it should have been so done. It would be claim-
ing too much for ourselves not to concede to God that he may have
reasons for his plan that are hidden from us.   II, xi, 14

Since the advent of Christ, God's call has gone forth more widely
through all peoples, and the graces of the Spirit have been more
abundantly poured out than before. Who then, I pray, will say it is
not meet that God should have in his own hand and will the free
disposing of his graces, and should illuminate such nations as he
wills? To evoke the preaching of his Word at such places as he
wills? To give progress and success to his doctrine in such way and
measure as he wills? To deprive the world, because of its ungratefulness, of the knowledge of his name for such ages as he wills, and

according to his mercy to restore it when he again wills? We see
these, then, as too disgraceful slanders, used by impious men to
trouble the simple-minded and to make them doubt either the
righteousness of God or the trustworthiness of Scripture.

II, xi, 14

GOD, EXISTENCE OF

There is within the human mind, and indeed by natural instinct,
an awareness of divinity. This we take to be beyond controversy.

I, iii, 1

GOD, FAITHFULNESS OF

Even if all men are liars and faithless, still God does not cease to
be trustworthy.   IV, xv, 17

GOD, FORGIVENESS OF

And this which I have just said ought to be applied as an example
for the others in order that we may learn more readily to apply
our minds and our efforts to sincere repentance, because there must
be no doubt that when we are truly and heartily converted, God,
who extends his mercy even to the unworthy when they show any
dissatisfaction with self, will readily forgive us.   III, iii, 25

GOD, GOODNESS OF

This I take to mean that not only does he sustain this universe (as
he once founded it) by his boundless might, regulate it by his wisdom, preserve it by his goodness, and especially rule mankind by
his righteousness and judgment, bear with it in his mercy, watch
over it by his protection; but also that no drop will be found either
of wisdom and light, or of righteousness or power or rectitude, or of
genuine truth, which does not flow from him, and of which he is not
the cause. Thus we may learn to await and seek all these things from
him, and thankfully to ascribe them, once received, to him.

I, ii, 1

Furthermore, if the cause is sought by which he was led once to create all these things, and is now moved to preserve them, we shall find that it is his goodness alone. But this being the sole cause, it ought still to be more than sufficient to draw us to his love, inasmuch as there is no creature, as the prophet declares, upon whom God's mercy has not been poured out.   I, v, 6

David exclaims that infants still nursing at their mothers' breasts are eloquent enough to celebrate God's glory, for immediately on coming forth from the womb, they find food prepared for them by his heavenly care. Indeed, this is in general true, provided what experience plainly demonstrates does not escape our eyes and senses, that some mothers have full and abundant breasts, but others' are almost dry, as God wills to feed one more liberally, but another more meagerly.   I, xvi, 3

GOD, IDEA OF
From this, my present contention is brought out with greater certainty, that a sense of divinity is by nature engraven on human hearts. For necessity forces from the reprobate themselves a confession of it.   I, iv, 4

GOD, IMAGE OF
And although the primary seat of the divine image was in the mind and heart, or in the soul and its powers, yet there was no part of man, not even the body itself, in which some sparks did not glow. . . .
Then in the thing itself there is no ambiguity, simply man is called God's image because he is like God.
Therefore, although the soul is not man, yet it is not absurd for man, in respect to his soul, to be called God's image; even though I retain the principle I just now set forward, that the likeness of God extends to the whole excellence by which man's nature towers over all the kinds of living creatures.   I, xv, 3

Now we are to see what Paul chiefly comprehends under this renewal. In the first place he posits knowledge, then pure righteousness and holiness. From this we infer that, to begin with, God's image was visible in the light of the mind, in the uprightness of the heart, and in the soundness of all the parts.

Now we see how Christ is the most perfect image of God; if we are conformed to it, we are so restored that with true piety, righteousness, purity, and intelligence we bear God's image.   I, xv, 4

At that time, I say, when he had been advanced to the highest degree of honor, Scripture attributed nothing else to him than that he had been created in the image of God, thus suggesting that man was blessed, not because of his own good actions, but by participation in God.   II, ii, 1

Assuredly there is but one way in which to achieve what is not merely difficult but utterly against human nature: to love those who hate us, to repay their evil deeds with benefits, to return blessings for reproaches. It is that we remember not to consider men's evil intention but to look upon the image of God in them, which cancels and effaces their transgressions, and with its beauty and dignity allures us to love and embrace them.   III, vii, 6

GOD, JEALOUSY OF

God is provoked to jealousy as often as we substitute our own inventions in place of him. This is like a shameless woman who brings in an adulterer before her husband's very eyes only to vex his mind the more.   II, viii, 16

God very commonly takes on the character of a husband to us. Indeed, the union by which he binds us to himself when he receives us into the bosom of the church is like sacred wedlock, which must rest upon mutual faithfulness. As he performs all the duties of a true and faithful husband, of us in return he demands love and conjugal chastity. That is, we are not to yield our souls to Satan, to lust, and to the filthy desires of the flesh, to be defiled by them.
    II, viii, 18

GOD, KINGDOM OF

But even though the definition of this Kingdom was put before us previously, I now briefly repeat it: God reigns where men, both by denial of themselves and by contempt of the world and of earthly life, pledge themselves to his righteousness in order to aspire to a heavenly life.   III, xx, 42

GOD, KNOWLEDGE OF

Let us use great caution that neither our thoughts nor our speech go beyond the limits to which the Word of God itself extends. For how can the human mind measure off the measureless essence of God according to its own little measure, a mind as yet unable to establish for certain the nature of the sun's body, though men's eyes daily gaze upon it? Indeed, how can the mind by its own leading come to search out God's essence when it cannot even get to its own? Let us then willingly leave to God the knowledge of himself.

I, xiii, 21

GOD, LOVE OF

Indeed, no one gives himself freely and willingly to God's service unless, having tasted his fatherly love, he is drawn to love and worship him in return.   I, v, 3

Here, however, the foul ungratefulness of men is disclosed. They have within themselves a workshop graced with God's unnumbered works and, at the same time, a storehouse overflowing with inestimable riches. They ought, then, to break forth into praises of him but are actually puffed up and swollen with all the more pride.

I, v, 4

"God's love," says he [Augustine], "is incomprehensible and unchangeable. For it was not after we were reconciled to him through the blood of his Son that he began to love us. Rather, he has loved us before the world was created, that we also might be his sons along with his only-begotten Son—before we became anything at all. The fact that we were reconciled through Christ's death must not be understood as if his Son reconciled us to him that he might now begin to love those whom he had hated. Rather, we have already been reconciled to him who loves us, with whom we were enemies on account of sin." II, xvi, 4

GOD, MERCY OF

For who even of slight intelligence does not understand that, as nurses commonly do with infants, God is wont in a measure to "lisp" in speaking to us? Thus such forms of speaking do not so much express clearly what God is like as accommodate the knowledge of him to our slight capacity. To do this he must descend far beneath his loftiness. I, xiii, 1

For in what way does true faith justify save when it binds us to Christ so that, made one with him, we may enjoy participation in his righteousness? It therefore justifies not because it grasps a knowledge of God's essence but because it rests upon the assurance of his mercy. III, xvii, 11

For God, as has been seen above, declaring that he will be gentle and kind to all, gives to the utterly miserable, hope that they will get what they have sought. Accordingly, we must note the general forms, by which no one from first to last (as people say) is excluded, provided sincerity of heart, dissatisfaction with ourselves, humility, and faith are present in order that our hypocrisy may not profane God's name by calling upon him deceitfully. Our most gracious Father will not cast out those whom he not only urges, but stirs up with every possible means, to come to him. III, xx, 14

GOD, NATURE AND

I confess, of course, that it can be said reverently, provided that it proceeds from a reverent mind, that nature is God; but because it is a harsh and improper saying, since nature is rather the order prescribed by God, it is harmful in such weighty matters, in which special devotion is due, to involve God confusedly in the inferior course of his works. I, v, 5

GOD, NATURE OF

Just so, an eye to which nothing is shown but black objects judges
something dirty white or even rather darkly mottled to be white-
ness itself. Indeed, we can discern still more clearly from the bodily
senses how much we are deluded in estimating the powers of the
soul. For if in broad daylight we either look down upon the ground
or survey whatever meets our view round about, we seem to ourselves endowed with the strongest and keenest sight; yet when we
look up to the sun and gaze straight at it, that power of sight which
was particularly strong on earth is at once blunted and confused by
a great brilliance, and thus we are compelled to admit that our
keenness in looking upon things earthly is sheer dullness when it
comes to the sun. So it happens in estimating our spiritual goods.
As long as we do not look beyond the earth, being quite content
with our own righteousness, wisdom, and virtue, we flatter ourselves most sweetly, and fancy ourselves all but demigods. Suppose
we but once begin to raise our thoughts to God, and to ponder his
nature, and how completely perfect are his righteousness, wisdom,
and power—the straightedge to which we must be shaped. Then,
what masquerading earlier as righteousness was pleasing in us will
soon grow filthy in its consummate wickedness. What wonderfully
impressed us under the name of wisdom will stink in its very foolishness. What wore the face of power will prove itself the most
miserable weakness. That is, what in us seems perfection itself corresponds ill to the purity of God.   I, i, 2

GOD, PERFECTION OF

Thus, from the feeling of our own ignorance, vanity, poverty, infirmity, and—what is more—depravity and corruption, we recognize
that the true light of wisdom, sound virtue, full abundance of every
good, and purity of righteousness rest in the Lord alone.   I, i, 1

GOD, PROVIDENCE OF

To conclude once for all, whenever we call God the Creator of
heaven and earth, let us at the same time bear in mind that the
dispensation of all those things which he has made is in his own

hand and power and that we are indeed his children, whom he has received into his faithful protection to nourish and educate. We are therefore to await the fullness of all good things from him alone and to trust completely that he will never leave us destitute of what we need for salvation, and to hang our hopes on none but him! We are therefore, also, to petition him for whatever we desire; and we are to recognize as a blessing from him, and thankfully to acknowledge, every benefit that falls to our share. So, invited by the great sweetness of his beneficence and goodness, let us study to love and serve him with all our heart.   I, xiv, 22

GOD, POWER OF

With what clear manifestations his might draws us to contemplate him! Unless perchance it be unknown to us in whose power it lies to sustain this infinite mass of heaven and earth by his Word: by his nod alone sometimes to shake heaven with thunderbolts, to burn everything with lightnings, to kindle the air with flashes; sometimes to disturb it with various sorts of storms, and then at his pleasure to clear them away in a moment; to compel the sea, which by its height seems to threaten the earth with continual destruction, to hang as if in mid-air; sometimes to arouse it in a dreadful way with the tumultuous force of winds; sometimes, with waves quieted, to make it calm again!   I, v, 6

GOD, PURITY OF

For if the stars, which seem so very bright at night, lose their brilliance in the sight of the sun, what do we think will happen even to the rarest innocence of man when it is compared with God's purity?   III, xii, 4

GOD, UNIVERSALITY OF BELIEF IN

Yet there is, as the eminent pagan says, no nation so barbarous, no people so savage, that they have not a deep-seated conviction that there is a God.   I, iii, 1

GOD, WAY OF KNOWING

Consequently, we know the most perfect way of seeking God, and the most suitable order, is not for us to attempt with bold curiosity to penetrate to the investigation of his essence, which we ought more to adore than meticulously to search out, but for us to contemplate him in his works whereby he renders himself near and familiar to us, and in some manner communicates himself.   I, v, 9

GOD, WILL OF

The will of God is unchangeable, I admit, and his truth ever remains in agreement with itself. Yet I deny that the reprobate proceed so far as to penetrate into that secret revelation which Scripture vouchsafes only to the elect. I deny, therefore, that they either grasp the will of God as it is immutable, or steadfastly embrace its truth, for they tarry in but a fleeting awareness. They are like a tree not planted deep enough to put down living roots. For some years it may put forth not only blossoms and leaves, but even fruits; nevertheless, it withers after the passage of time.   III, ii, 12

GOD, WISDOM OF

When dense clouds darken the sky, and a violent tempest arises, because a gloomy mist is cast over our eyes, thunder strikes our ears and all our senses are benumbed with fright, everything seems to us to be confused and mixed up; but all the while a constant quiet and serenity ever remain in heaven. So must we infer that, while the disturbances in the world deprive us of judgment, God out of the pure light of his justice and wisdom tempers and directs these very movements in the best-conceived order to a right end.   I, xvii, 1

GOD, WORKS OF

Indeed, his essence is incomprehensible; hence, his divineness far escapes all human perception. But upon his individual works he has engraved unmistakable marks of his glory, so clear and so prominent that even unlettered and stupid folk cannot plead the excuse of ignorance. . . . Yet, in the first place, wherever you cast your eyes, there is no spot in the universe wherein you cannot discern at least some sparks of his glory. You cannot in one glance survey this most vast and beautiful system of the universe, in its wide expanse, without being completely overwhelmed by the boundless force of its brightness.   I, v, 1

But although the Lord represents both himself and his everlasting Kingdom in the mirror of his works with very great clarity, such is our stupidity that we grow increasingly dull toward so manifest testimonies, and they flow away without profiting us. For with regard to the most beautiful structure and order of the universe, how many of us are there who, when we lift up our eyes to heaven or cast them about through the various regions of earth, recall our minds to a remembrance of the Creator, and do not rather, disregarding their Author, sit idly in contemplation of his works?

I, v, 11

Nobody seriously believes the universe was made by God without being persuaded that he takes care of his works.   I, xvi, 1

No creature has a force more wondrous or glorious than that of the sun. For besides lighting the whole earth with its brightness, how great a thing is it that by its heat it nourishes and quickens all living things! That with its rays it breathes fruitfulness into the earth! That it warms the seeds in the bosom of the earth, draws them forth with budding greenness, increases and strengthens them, nourishes them anew, until they rise up into stalks! That it feeds the plant with continual warmth, until it grows into flower, and from flower into fruit! That then, also with baking heat it brings the fruit to maturity! That in like manner trees and vines warmed by the sun first put forth buds and leaves, then put forth a flower, and from the flower produce fruit! Yet the Lord, to claim the whole credit for all these things, willed that, before he created the sun, light should come to be and earth be filled with all manner of herbs and fruits. Therefore a godly man will not make the sun either the principal or the necessary cause of these things which existed before the creation of the sun, but merely the instrument that God uses because he so wills; for with no more difficulty he might abandon it, and act through himself.   I, xvi, 2

GOOD
To sum up, much as man desires to follow what is good, still he does not follow it.   II, ɪɪ, 26

God's goodness is so connected with his divinity that it is no more necessary for him to be God than for him to be good.   II, ɪɪɪ, 5

GOSPEL
Now I take the gospel to be the clear manifestation of the mystery of Christ.   II, ɪx, 2

GOVERNMENT, AUTHORITY OF
For since the church does not have the power to coerce, and ought not to seek it (I am speaking of civil coercion), it is the duty of godly kings and princes to sustain religion by laws, edicts, and judgments.   IV, xɪ, 16

GOVERNMENT, END OF
Now, that king who in ruling over his realm does not serve God's glory exercises not kingly rule but brigandage. Furthermore, he is deceived who looks for enduring prosperity in his kingdom when it is not ruled by God's scepter, that is, his Holy Word; for the heavenly oracle that proclaims that "where prophecy fails the people are scattered" cannot lie.   DEDICATION

GOVERNMENT, FORMS OF
And if you compare the forms of government among themselves apart from the circumstances, it is not easy to distinguish which one of them excels in usefulness, for they contend on such equal terms. The fall from kingdom to tyranny is easy; but it is not much more difficult to fall from the rule of the best men to the faction of a few; yet it is easiest of all to fall from popular rule to sedition. For if the three forms of government which the philosophers discuss be considered in themselves, I will not deny that aristocracy, or a system compounded of aristocracy and democracy, far excels all

others: not indeed of itself, but because it is very rare for kings so to control themselves that their will never disagrees with what is just and right; or for them to have been endowed with such great keenness and prudence, that each knows how much is enough. Therefore, men's fault or failing causes it to be safer and more bearable for a number to exercise government, so that they may help one another, teach and admonish one another; and, if one asserts himself unfairly, there may be a number of censors and masters to restrain his willfulness.   IV, xx, 8

GOVERNMENT, FUNCTIONS OF

For from experience we thoroughly agree with the statement of Solon that all commonwealths are maintained by reward and punishment; take these away and the whole discipline of cities collapses and is dissolved. For the care of equity and justice grows cold in the minds of many, unless due honor has been prepared for virtue; and the lust of wicked men cannot be restrained except by severity and the infliction of penalties.   IV, xx, 9

GOVERNMENT, GOD AND

But in that obedience which we have shown to be due the authority of rulers, we are always to make this exception, indeed, to observe it as primary, that such obedience is never to lead us away from obedience to him, to whose will the desires of all kings ought to be subject, to whose decrees all their commands ought to yield, to whose majesty their scepters ought to be submitted. And how absurd would it be that in satisfying men you should incur the displeasure of him for whose sake you obey men themselves! The Lord, therefore, is the King of Kings, who, when he has opened his sacred mouth, must alone be heard, before all and above all men; next to him we are subject to those men who are in authority over us, but only in him. If they command anything against him, let it go unesteemed.   IV, xx, 32

GOVERNMENT, KINDS OF

Therefore, in order that none of us may stumble on that stone, let us first consider that there is a twofold government in man: one aspect is spiritual, whereby the conscience is instructed in piety and in reverencing God; the second is political, whereby man is educated for the duties of humanity and citizenship that must be maintained among men.   III, xix, 15

GOVERNMENT, LAXITY OF
For during the reign of Nerva it was not without reason said: it is indeed bad to live under a prince with whom nothing is permitted; but much worse under one by whom everything is allowed.

IV, xx, 10

GOVERNMENT, MAGISTRATE AND
For we must consider that the magistrate's revenge is not man's but God's, which he extends and exercises, as Paul says, through the ministry of man for our good.   IV, xx, 19

I am not discussing the men themselves, as if a mask of dignity covered foolishness, or sloth, or cruelty, as well as wicked morals full of infamous deeds, and thus acquired for vices the praise of virtues; but I say that the order itself is worthy of such honor and reverence that those who are rulers are esteemed among us, and receive reverence out of respect for their lordship.   IV, xx, 22

GOVERNMENT, OBEDIENCE TO
For this reason let a people hold all its rulers in honor, patiently bearing their government, obeying their laws and commands, refusing nothing that can be borne without losing God's favor. Again, let the rulers take care of their own common people, keep the public peace, protect the good, punish the evil. So let them manage all things as if they are about to render account of their services to God, the supreme Judge.   II, viii, 46

GOVERNMENT, RULERS OF
If we have continually present to our minds and before our eyes the fact that even the most worthless kings are appointed by the

same decree by which the authority of all kings is established, those seditious thoughts will never enter our minds that a king should be treated according to his merits, and that it is unfair that we should show ourselves subjects to him who, on his part, does not show himself a king to us.   IV, xx, 27

GOVERNMENT, WORD AND

But if we look to God's Word, it will lead us farther. We are not only subject to the authority of princes who perform their office toward us uprightly and faithfully as they ought, but also to the authority of all who, by whatever means, have got control of affairs, even though they perform not a whit of the princes' office.

IV, xx, 25

GRACE

On the other hand, it behooves us to consider the sort of remedy by which divine grace corrects and cures the corruption of nature. . . . God begins his good work in us, therefore, by arousing love and desire and zeal for righteousness in our hearts; or, to speak more correctly, by bending, forming, and directing, our hearts to righteousness. He completes his work, moreover, by confirming us to perseverance.   II, III, 6

GRACE, CHRIST'S WORK IN

I reply that "accepting grace," as they call it, is nothing else than his free goodness, with which the Father embraces us in Christ when he clothes us with the innocence of Christ and accepts it as ours that by the benefit of it he may hold us as holy, pure, and innocent.

III, xiv, 12

GRACE, HOLY SPIRIT AND

And thus when God teaches not through the letter of the law but through the grace of the Spirit, He so teaches that whatever anyone has learned he not only sees by knowing, but also seeks by willing, and achieves by doing.   II, III, 7

GRACE, LAW AND

Augustine often speaks of the value of calling upon the grace of His help. For example he writes . . . to Innocent of Rome: "The law commands; grace supplies the strength to act."   II, vii, 9

GRACE, LIBERTY AND

To be Christians under the law of grace does not mean to wander unbridled outside the law, but to be engrafted in Christ, by whose grace we are free of the curse of the law, and by whose Spirit we have the law engraved upon our hearts.   II, viii, 57

GRACE, RIGHTEOUSNESS AND

Therefore, we must come to this remedy: that believers should be convinced that their only ground of hope for the inheritance of a Heavenly Kingdom lies in the fact that, being engrafted in the body of Christ, they are freely accounted righteous. For, as regards justification, faith is something merely passive, bringing nothing of ours to the recovering of God's favor but receiving from Christ that which we lack.   III, xiii, 5

GRACE, WITHDRAWING OF GOD'S

God sometimes, having withdrawn the assistance of his grace, tries men and waits to see to what purpose they will turn their efforts.   II, v, 13

GRACE, WORKS AND

Now we have from Augustine's own lips the testimony that we especially wish to obtain: not only is grace offered by the Lord, which by anyone's free choice may be accepted or rejected; but it is this very grace which forms both choice and will in the heart, so that whatever good works then follow are the fruit and effect of grace; and it has no other will obeying it except the will that it has made. There are also Augustine's words from another place: "Grace alone brings about every good work in us."   II, iii, 13

HAPPINESS

Even poverty, if it be judged in itself, is misery; likewise exile, contempt, prison, disgrace; finally, death itself is the ultimate of all calamities. But when the favor of our God breathes upon us, every one of these things turns into happiness for us.   III, viii, 7

HEART

The human heart has so many crannies where vanity hides, so many holes where falsehood lurks, is so decked out with deceiving hypocrisy, that it often dupes itself.   III, ii, 10

Whoever is moderately versed in Scripture will understand by himself, without the admonition of another, that when we have to deal with God nothing is achieved unless we begin from the inner disposition of the heart.   III, iii, 16

HEAVEN

For few out of a huge multitude care how they are to go to heaven, but all long to know beforehand what takes place there.
                                                        III, xxv, 11

HEAVEN, CHRIST'S WORK IN

Secondly, as faith recognizes, it is to our great benefit that Christ resides with the Father. For, having entered a sanctuary not made with hands, he appears before the Father's face as our constant advocate and intercessor. Thus he turns the Father's eyes to his own righteousness to avert his gaze from our sins. He so reconciles the Father's heart to us that by his intercession he prepares a way and access for us to the Father's throne. He fills with grace and kindness the throne that for miserable sinners would otherwise have been filled with dread.   II, xvi, 16

HEAVEN, KINGDOM OF

The use of the term "reward" is no reason for us to suppose that our works are the cause of our salvation. First, let us be heartily convinced that the Kingdom of Heaven is not servants' wages but sons' inheritance, which only they who have been adopted as sons by the Lord shall enjoy, and that for no other reason than this adoption.   III, xviii, 2

HEAVEN, PREPARATION FOR

We ought, then, to imitate what people do who determine to migrate to another place, where they have chosen a lasting abode. They send before them all their resources and do not grieve over lacking them for a time, for they deem themselves the happier the more goods they have where they will be for a long time. But if we believe heaven is our country, it is better to transmit our possessions thither than to keep them here where upon our sudden migration they would be lost to us.   III, xviii, 6

HELL

Besides, this mind restrains itself from sinning, not out of dread of punishment alone; but, because it loves and reveres God as Father, it worships and adores him as Lord. Even if there were no hell, it would still shudder at offending him alone.   I, ii, 2

And surely no more terrible abyss can be conceived than to feel yourself forsaken and estranged from God; and when you call upon him, not to be heard. It is as if God himself had plotted your ruin.   II, xvi, 11

HELL, DESCENT INTO

But we must seek a surer explanation, apart from the Creed, of Christ's descent into hell. The explanation given to us in God's Word is not only holy and pious, but also full of wonderful consolation. If Christ had died only a bodily death, it would have been ineffectual. No—it was expedient at the same time for him to undergo the severity of God's vengeance, to appease his wrath and satisfy his just judgment. For this reason, he must also grapple hand to hand with the armies of hell and the dread of everlasting death. A little while ago we referred to the prophet's statement that "the chastisement of our peace was laid upon him," "he was wounded for our transgressions" by the Father, "he was bruised for our infirmities." By these words he means that Christ was put in place of evildoers as surety and pledge—submitting himself even as the accused—to bear and suffer all the punishments that they ought to have sustained. All—with this one exception: "He could not be held by the pangs of death." No wonder, then, if he is said to have descended into hell, for he suffered the death that God in his wrath had inflicted upon the wicked! Those who—on the ground that it is absurd to put after his burial what preceded it—say that the order is reversed in this way are making a very trifling and ridiculous objection. The point is that the Creed sets forth what Christ suffered in the sight of men, and then appositely speaks of that invisible and incomprehensible judgment which he underwent in the sight of God in order that we might know not only that Christ's body was given as the price of our redemption, but that he paid a greater and more excellent price in suffering in his soul the terrible torments of a condemned and forsaken man.   II, xvi, 10

HOLY DAYS

Christians ought therefore to shun completely the superstitious observance of days. . . . Why do we not assemble daily, you ask, so as to remove all distinction of days? If only this had been given us! Spiritual wisdom truly deserved to have some portion of time set apart for it each day. But if the weakness of many made it impossible for daily meetings to be held, and the rule of love does not allow more to be required of them, why should we not obey the order we see laid upon us by God's will?   II, viii, 31–32

HOLY DAYS, SUPERSTITION IN

Nor do I cling to the number "seven" so as to bind the church in subjection to it. And I shall not condemn churches that have other solemn days for their meetings, provided there be no superstition.

II, viii, 34

HOLY SPIRIT, CHRIST AND THE

To sum up, the Holy Spirit is the bond by which Christ effectu-
ally unites us to himself.   III, i, 1

And, as the proper office of the Spirit, he assigned the task of
bringing to mind what he had taught by mouth. For light would be
given the sightless in vain had that Spirit of discernment not opened
the eyes of the mind. Consequently, he may rightly be called the key
that unlocks for us the treasures of the Kingdom of Heaven; and
his illumination, the keenness of our insight. Paul so highly com-
mends the "ministry of the Spirit" for the reason that teachers
would shout to no effect if Christ himself, inner Schoolmaster, did
not by his Spirit draw to himself those given to him by the Father.
We have said that perfect salvation is found in the person of Christ.
Accordingly, that we may become partakers of it "he baptizes us in
the Holy Spirit and fire," bringing us into the light of faith in his
gospel and so regenerating us that we become new creatures; and
he consecrates us, purged of worldly uncleanness, as temples holy to
God.   III, i, 4

HOLY SPIRIT, FAITH AND THE

I certainly admit to them that faith is the proper and entire work
of the Holy Spirit, illumined by whom we recognize God and the
treasures of his kindness, and without whose light our mind is so
blinded that it can see nothing; so dull that it can sense nothing of
spiritual things.   IV, xiv, 8

HOLY SPIRIT, ILLUMINATION OF THE

But I reply: the testimony of the Spirit is more excellent than all
reason. For as God alone is a fit witness of himself in his Word, so
also the Word will not find acceptance in men's hearts before it is
sealed by the inward testimony of the Spirit. The same Spirit,
therefore, who has spoken through the mouths of the prophets
must penetrate into our hearts to persuade us that they faithfully
proclaimed what had been divinely commanded. Isaiah very aptly
expresses this connection in these words: "My Spirit which is in
you, and the words that I have put in your mouth, and the mouths

of your offspring, shall never fail." Some good folk are annoyed that a clear proof is not ready at hand when the impious, unpunished, murmur against God's Word. As if the Spirit were not called both "seal" and "guarantee" for confirming the faith of the godly; because until he illumines their minds, they ever waver among many doubts! I, vii, 4

It therefore remains for us to understand that the way to the Kingdom of God is open only to him whose mind has been made new by the illumination of the Holy Spirit. II, ii, 20

HOLY SPIRIT, IMPROPERLY RECEIVED

The ceremonies admirably correspond to the reality. Our Lord, when he sent forth the apostles to preach the gospel, breathed upon them. By this symbol he represented the power of the Holy Spirit, which he gave them. These good men have retained this insufflation, and, as if they are putting forth the Holy Spirit from their throat, they mutter over those whom they are making priestlings, "Receive the Holy Spirit." They leave nothing which they do not preposterously counterfeit: I do not say like actors whose gestures have some art and meaning, but like apes, which imitate everything wantonly and without any discrimination. IV, xix, 29

HOLY SPIRIT, NATURE OF THE

For Christians the Spirit of the Lord is not a disturbing apparition, which they have either brought forth in a dream or have received as fashioned by others. Rather, they earnestly seek a knowledge of him from the Scriptures, where these two things are taught concerning him. First, he has been given to us for sanctification in order that he may bring us, purged of uncleanness and defilement, into obedience to God's righteousness. This obedience cannot stand except when the inordinate desires to which these men would slacken the reins have been tamed and subjugated. Second, we are purged by his sanctification in such a way that we are besieged by many vices and much weakness so long as we are encumbered with our body. Thus it comes about that, far removed from perfection, we must move steadily forward, and though entangled in vices, daily fight against them. From this it also follows that we must shake off sloth and carelessness, and watch with intent minds lest, unaware, we be overwhelmed by the stratagems of our flesh. Unless, perchance, we are confident that we have made greater progress than the apostle, who was still harassed by an angel of Satan "whereby his power was made perfect in weakness," and who in his own flesh unfeignedly represented that division between flesh and spirit.

III, III, 14

HOLY SPIRIT, RESURRECTION AND THE

Now, that our fellowship with Christ in the blessed resurrection may not be doubtful, in order that we may be content with this pledge, Paul plainly declares that Christ is seated in heaven, and will come on the Last Day as judge to conform our lowly, inglorious body to his glorious body.   III, xxv, 3

HOLY SPIRIT, SACRAMENTS AND THE

For as we do not doubt that Christ's body is limited by the general characteristics common to all human bodies, and is contained in heaven (where it was once for all received) until Christ return in judgment, so we deem it utterly unlawful to draw it back under these corruptible elements or to imagine it to be present everywhere. And there is no need of this for us to enjoy a participation in it, since the Lord bestows this benefit upon us through his Spirit so that we may be made one in body, spirit, and soul with him. The bond of this connection is therefore the Spirit of Christ, with whom we are joined in unity, and is like a channel through which all that Christ himself is and has is conveyed to us. For if we see that the sun, shedding its beams upon the earth, casts its substance in some measure upon it in order to beget, nourish, and give growth to its offspring—why should the radiance of Christ's Spirit be less in order to impart to us the communion of his flesh and blood? On this account, Scripture, in speaking of our participation with Christ, relates its whole power to the Spirit.   IV, xvii, 12

HOLY SPIRIT, SILENCE OF THE

And in fact, while the Spirit ever teaches us to our profit, he either remains absolutely silent upon those things of little value for edification, or only lightly and cursorily touches them. It is also our duty willingly to renounce those things which are unprofitable.

I, XIV, 3

HOLY SPIRIT, SIN AGAINST THE

I say, therefore, that they sin against the Holy Spirit who, with evil intention, resist God's truth, although by its brightness they are so touched that they cannot claim ignorance. Such resistance alone constitutes this sin.   III, III, 22

HOLY SPIRIT, TITLES OF THE

And here it is useful to note what titles are applied to the Holy Spirit in Scripture, when the beginning and the whole renewal of our salvation are under discussion. First, he is called the "spirit of adoption" because he is the witness to us of the free benevolence of God with which God the Father has embraced us in his beloved only-begotten Son to become a Father to us; and he encourages us to have trust in prayer. In fact, he supplies the very words so that we may fearlessly cry, "Abba, Father!" For the same reason he is called "the guarantee and seal" of our inheritance because from heaven he so gives life to us, on pilgrimage in the world and resembling dead men, as to assure us that our salvation is safe in God's unfailing care. He is also called "life" because of righteousness. By his secret watering the Spirit makes us fruitful to bring forth the buds of righteousness. Accordingly, he is frequently called "water," as in Isaiah: "Come, all ye who thirst, to the waters." Also, "I shall pour out my Spirit upon him who thirsts, and rivers upon the dry land." To these verses Christ's statement, quoted above, corresponds: "If anyone thirst, let him come to me." Although sometimes he is so called because of his power to cleanse and purify, as in Ezekiel, where the Lord promises "clean water" in which he will "wash away the filth" of his people. From the fact that he restores and nourishes unto vigor of life those on whom he has poured the stream of his grace, he gets the names "oil" and "anointing." On the other hand, persistently boiling away and burning up our vicious and inordinate desires, he enflames our hearts with the love of God and with zealous devotion. From this effect upon us he is also justly called "fire." In short, he is described as the "spring" whence all heavenly riches flow forth to us; or as the "hand of God," by which he exercises his might. For by the inspiration of his power he so breathes divine life into us that we are no longer actuated by ourselves, but are ruled by his action and prompting. Accordingly, whatever good things are in us are the fruits of his grace; and without him our gifts are darkness of mind and perversity of heart. As has already been clearly explained, until our minds become intent upon the Spirit, Christ, so to speak, lies idle because we coldly contemplate him as outside ourselves—indeed, far from us. We know, moreover, that he benefits only those whose "Head" he is, for whom he is "the first-born among brethren," and who, finally, "have put on him." This union alone ensures that, as far as we are concerned, he has not unprofitably come with the name of Savior.   III, i, 3

HOLY SPIRIT, WORD AND THE

And this bare and external proof of the Word of God should have been amply sufficient to engender faith, did not our blindness and perversity prevent it. But our mind has such an inclination to vanity that it can never cleave fast to the truth of God; and it has such a dullness that it is always blind to the light of God's truth.

II, ii, 33

HOLY SPIRIT, WORK OF THE

Thus through him we come into communion with God, so that we in a way feel his life-giving power toward us. Our justification is his work; from him is power, sanctification, truth, grace, and every good thing that can be conceived, since there is but one Spirit from whom flows every sort of gift.   I, xiii, 14

HONOR
I consider it no honor to see the honor of my brethren diminished. For my honor is the honor of the church universal, and the life and vigor of my brethren.   IV, vii, 16

HOPE
Although, therefore, Christ offers us in the gospel a present fullness of spiritual benefits, the enjoyment thereof ever lies hidden under the guardianship of hope, until, having put off corruptible flesh, we be transfigured in the glory of him who goes before us.

II, ix, 3

HUMAN RESPONSIBILITY
For he who has set the limits to our life has at the same time entrusted to us its care; he has provided means and helps to preserve it; he has also made us able to foresee dangers; that they may not overwhelm us unaware, he has offered precautions and remedies. Now it is very clear what our duty is: thus, if the Lord has committed to us the protection of our life, our duty is to protect it; if he offers helps, to use them; if he forewarns us of dangers, not to plunge headlong; if he makes remedies available, not to neglect them.   I, xvii, 4

HUMILITY
Therefore no one will weigh God's providence properly and profitably but him who considers that his business is with his Maker and the Framer of the universe, and with becoming humility submits himself to fear and reverence.   I, xvii, 2

First consider that the gateway to salvation does not lie open unless we have laid aside all pride and taken upon ourselves perfect humility; secondly, that this humility is not some seemly behavior whereby you yield a hair of your right to the Lord, as those who do not act haughtily or insult others are called humble in the sight of men, although they rely upon some consciousness of excellence. Rather, this humility is an unfeigned submission of our heart, stricken down in earnest with an awareness of its own misery and want. For so it is everywhere described by the Word of God.

III, xii, 6

IDOLATRY

Meanwhile, since this brute stupidity gripped the whole world —to pant after visible figures of God, and thus to form gods of wood, stone, gold, silver, or other dead and corruptible matter—we must cling to this principle: God's glory is corrupted by an impious falsehood whenever any form is attached to him.   I, xi, 1

Therefore, if the papists have any shame, let them henceforward not use this evasion, that pictures are the books of the uneducated, because it is plainly refuted by very many testimonies of Scripture. Even if I were to grant them this, yet they would not thus gain much to defend their idols. It is well known that they set monstrosities of this kind in place of God. The pictures or statues that they dedicate to saints—what are they but examples of the most abandoned lust and obscenity? If anyone wished to model himself after them, he would be fit for the lash. Indeed, brothels show harlots clad more virtuously and modestly than the churches show those objects which they wish to be thought images of virgins. For martyrs they fashion a habit not a whit more decent. Therefore let them compose their idols at least to a moderate decency, that they may with a little more modesty falsely claim that these are books of some holiness! But then we shall also answer that this is not the method of teaching within the sacred precincts believing folk, whom God wills to be instructed there with a far different doctrine than this trash. In the preaching of his Word and sacred mysteries he has bidden that a common doctrine be there set forth for all. But those whose eyes rove about in contemplating idols betray that their minds are not diligently intent upon this doctrine.   I, xi, 7

But even if so much danger were not threatening, when I ponder the intended use of churches, somehow or other it seems to me unworthy of their holiness for them to take on images other than those living and symbolical ones which the Lord has consecrated by his Word. I mean Baptism and the Lord's Supper, together with other rites by which our eyes must be too intensely gripped and too sharply affected to seek other images forged by human ingenuity.   I, xi, 13

IMMORTALITY

Knowledge of this sort, then, ought not only to arouse us to the worship of God but also to awaken and encourage us to the hope of the future life. For since we notice that the examples that the Lord shows us both of his clemency and of his severity are inchoate and incomplete, doubtless we must consider this to presage even greater things, the manifestation and full exhibition of which are deferred to another life.   I, v, 10

Therefore, he [Augustine] bears witness that all godly men, no less than prophets, apostles, and martyrs, immediately after death enjoy blessed repose. If such is their condition, what, I beg of you, will our prayers confer upon them?   III, v, 10

But, nothing is more difficult than, having bidden farewell to the reason of the flesh and having bridled our desires—nay, having put them away—to devote ourselves to God and our brethren, and to meditate, amid earth's filth, upon the life of the angels. Consequently, Paul, in order to extricate our minds from all snares, recalls us to the hope of blessed immortality, reminding us that we strive not in vain. For, as Christ our Redeemer once appeared, so in his final coming he will show the fruit of the salvation brought forth by him.   III, vii, 3

Whatever kind of tribulation presses upon us, we must ever look to this end: to accustom ourselves to contempt for the present life and to be aroused thereby to meditate upon the future life.
     III, ix, 1

But let believers accustom themselves to a contempt of the present life that engenders no hatred of it or ingratitude against God. Indeed, this life, however crammed with infinite miseries it may be, is still rightly to be counted among those blessings of God which are not to be spurned. . . . And this is a much greater reason if in it we reflect that we are in preparation, so to speak, for the glory of the Heavenly Kingdom.   III, ix, 3

For if we deem this unstable, defective, corruptible, fleeting, wasting, rotting tabernacle of our body to be so dissolved that it is soon renewed unto a firm, perfect, incorruptible, and finally, heavenly glory, will not faith compel us ardently to seek what nature dreads? . . . Let us, however, consider this settled: that no one has made progress in the school of Christ who does not joyfully await the day of death and final resurrection.   III, ix, 5

INTEMPERANCE
He who bids you use this world as if you used it not destroys not only the intemperance of gluttony in food and drink, and excessive indulgence at table, in buildings and clothing, ambition, pride, arrogance, and overfastidiousness, but also all care and inclination that either diverts or hinders you from thought of the heavenly life and zeal to cultivate the soul.   III, x, 4

So he who conducts himself intemperately not only sins because he gives a bad example to his brothers but has a conscience bound by guilt before God.   III, xix, 16

INVECTIVE
Osiander considers these trivialities, which I have by now refuted, to be the firmest of oracles! Drunk with the sweetness of his own speculations, he is wont to intone his absurd paeans over nothing!   II, xii, 7

Now indulgences flow from this doctrine of satisfaction. For our opponents pretend that to make satisfaction those indulgences supply what our powers lack. And they go to the mad extreme of defining them as the distribution of the merits of Christ and the martyrs, which the pope distributes by his bulls. These men are fit to be treated by drugs for insanity rather than to be argued with.

For it is hardly worth-while to undertake to refute errors so foolish, which under the onslaught of many battering-rams are of themselves beginning to grow old and to show deterioration. But because a brief refutation will be useful for certain uninstructed persons, I shall not omit it.   III, v, 1

But Osiander, by spurning this spiritual bond, forces a gross mingling of Christ with believers. And for this reason, he maliciously calls "Zwinglian" all those who do not subscribe to his mad error of "essential righteousness" because they do not hold the view that Christ is eaten in substance in the Lord's Supper. I consider it the highest glory to be thus insulted by a proud man, and one entangled in his own deceits; albeit he attacks not only me but world-renowned writers whom he ought modestly to have respected.   III, xi, 10

JUDGMENT

Accordingly, whoever heedlessly indulges himself, his fear of heavenly judgment extinguished, denies that there is a God.

I, iv, 2

Let us, therefore, learn from this confession of David's that the holy patriarchs under the Old Testament were aware how rarely or never God fulfills in this world what he promises to his servants; and that they therefore lifted up their hearts to God's sanctuary, in which they found hidden what does not appear in the shadows of the present life. This place was the Last Judgment of God, which, although they could not discern it with their eyes, they were content to understand by faith.   II, x, 17

Hence arises a wonderful consolation: that we perceive judgment to be in the hands of him who has already destined us to share with him the honor of judging! Far indeed is he from mounting his judgment seat to condemn us! How could our most merciful Ruler destroy his people? How could the Head scatter his own members? How could our Advocate condemn his clients? For if the apostle dares exclaim that with Christ interceding for us there is no one who can come forth to condemn us, it is much more true, then, that Christ as Intercessor will not condemn those whom he has received into his charge and protection.   II, xvi, 18

JUSTICE

Where you hear God's glory mentioned, think of his justice. For whatever deserves praise must be just.   III, xxiii, 8

But here a seemingly hard and difficult question arises: if the law of God forbids all Christians to kill, and the prophet prophesies concerning God's holy mountain [the church] that in it men shall not afflict or hurt—how can magistrates be pious men and shedders of blood at the same time? Yet if we understand that the magistrate in administering punishments does nothing by himself, but carries out the very judgments of God, we shall not be hampered by this scruple. The law of the Lord forbids killing; but, that murders may not go unpunished, the Lawgiver himself puts into the hand of his ministers a sword to be drawn against all murderers. It is not for the pious to afflict and hurt; yet to avenge, at the Lord's command, the afflictions of the pious is not to hurt or to afflict. Would that this were ever before our minds—that nothing is done here from men's rashness, but all things are done on the authority of God who commands it; and while his authority goes before us, we never wander from the straight path!   IV, xx, 10

But if one is permitted to go to law with a brother, one is not therewith allowed to hate him, or be seized with a mad desire to harm him, or hound him relentlessly.   IV, xx, 17

For this must be a set principle for all Christians; that a lawsuit, however just, can never be rightly prosecuted by any man, unless he treat his adversary with the same love and good will as if the business under controversy were already amicably settled and composed. Perhaps someone will interpose here that such moderation is so uniformly absent from any lawsuit that it would be a miracle if any such were found. Indeed, I admit that, as the customs of these times go, an example of an upright litigant is rare; but the thing itself, when not corrupted by the addition of anything evil, does not cease to be good and pure.   IV, xx, 18

JUSTIFICATION BY FAITH

Therefore we must now discuss these matters [justification] thoroughly. And we must so discuss them as to bear in mind that this is the main hinge on which religion turns, so that we devote the greater attention and care to it.   III, xi, 1

Therefore, we explain justification simply as the acceptance with which God receives us into his favor as righteous men. And we say that it consists in the remission of sins and the imputation of Christ's righteousness.   III, xi, 2

Therefore, "to justify" means nothing else than to acquit of guilt him who was accused, as if his innocence were confirmed. Therefore, since God justifies us by the intercession of Christ, he absolves us not by the confirmation of our own innocence but by the imputation of righteousness, so that we who are not righteous in ourselves may be reckoned as such in Christ.   III, xi, 3

And although regenerated by the Spirit of God, he [the Christian] ponders the everlasting righteousness laid up for him not in the good works to which he inclines but in the sole righteousness of Christ.   III, xi, 16

To declare that by him alone we are accounted righteous, what else is this but to lodge our righteousness in Christ's obedience, because the obedience of Christ is reckoned to us as if it were our own?   III, xi, 23

The power of justifying, which faith possesses, does not lie in any worth of works. Our justification rests upon God's mercy alone and Christ's merit, and faith, when it lays hold of justification, is said to justify.   III, xviii, 8

KNOWLEDGE
Experience obviously teaches that until we put off the flesh we attain less than we should like. And in our daily reading of Scripture we come upon many obscure passages that convict us of ignorance. With this bridle God keeps us within bounds, assigning to each his "measure of faith" so that even the best teacher may be ready to learn.   III, ii, 4

LABOR
God, to prick our sloth, has given us the assurance that the trouble we have borne to the glory of his name will not be in vain. Let us always remember that this promise, like all others, would not bear fruit for us if the free covenant of his mercy had not gone before, upon which the whole assurance of our salvation depended. Now, relying on this, we ought to have firm confidence that, however unworthy our services, a reward will not be lacking from God's generosity.   III, xviii, 7

LAW, A MIRROR
The law is like a mirror. In it we contemplate our weakness, then the iniquity arising from this, and finally the curse coming from both—just as a mirror shows us the spots on our face.   II, vii, 7

LAW, CHRIST AND
It is very easy to refute this error. They have thought that Christ added to the law when he only restored it to its integrity, in that he freed and cleansed it when it had been obscured by the falsehoods and defiled by the leaven of the Pharisees.   II, viii, 7

Ceremonies are worthless and empty until the time of Christ is reached.   II, vii, 2

LAW, GOSPEL AND
Now the gospel differs from the law in that it does not link righteousness to works but lodges it solely in God's mercy.
III, xi, 18

LAW, INTERPRETATION OF

Therefore, plainly a sober interpretation of the law goes beyond the words; but just how far remains obscure unless some measure be set. Now, I think this would be the best rule, if attention be directed to the reason of the commandment; that is, in each commandment to ponder why it was given to us.   II, VIII, 8

LAW, MAGISTRATES AND

Next to the magistracy in the civil state come the laws, stoutest sinews of the commonwealth, or, as Cicero, after Plato, calls them, the souls, without which the magistracy cannot stand, even as they themselves have no force apart from the magistracy. Accordingly, nothing truer could be said than that the law is a silent magistrate; the magistrate, a living law.   IV, xx, 14

LAW, MOSES AND

I understand by the word "law" not only the Ten Commandments, which set forth a godly and righteous rule of living, but the form of religion handed down by God through Moses.   II, VII, 1

The law of Moses was wonderfully preserved by heavenly providence rather than by human effort.   I, VIII, 9

LAW, OBSERVANCE OF

Human laws, then, are satisfied when a man merely keeps his hand from wrongdoing. On the contrary, because the heavenly law has been given for our souls, they must at the outset be constrained, that it may be justly observed.   II, VIII, 6

LAW, PURPOSE OF

Now it will not be difficult to decide the purpose of the whole law: the fulfillment of righteousness to form human life to the archetype of divine purity.   II, VIII, 51

LAW, WEAKNESS OF

What point is there to see in the observance of the law the proffered reward of eternal life if, furthermore, it is not clear whether by this path we may attain eternal life. At this point the feebleness of the law shows itself. Because observance of the law is found in none of us, we are excluded from the promises of life, and fall back into the mere curse.   II, vii, 3

LIBERTY

But many today, while they seek an excuse for the intemperance of the flesh in its use of external things, and while they would meanwhile pave the road to licentious indulgence, take for granted what I do not at all concede to them: that this freedom is not to be restrained by any limitation but to be left to every man's conscience to use as far as seems lawful to him. Certainly I admit that consciences neither ought to nor can be bound here to definite and precise legal formulas; but inasmuch as Scripture gives general rules for lawful use, we ought surely to limit our use in accordance with them.   III, x, 1

Christian freedom, in my opinion, consists of three parts. The first: that the consciences of believers, in seeking assurance of their justification before God, should rise above and advance beyond the law, forgetting all law righteousness.   III, xix, 2

The second part, dependent upon the first, is that consciences observe the law, not as if constrained by the necessity of the law, but that freed from the law's yoke they willingly obey God's will.
III, xix, 4

The third part of Christian freedom lies in this: regarding outward things that are of themselves "indifferent," we are not bound before God by any religious obligation preventing us from sometimes using them and other times not using them, indifferently.
III, xix, 7

Accordingly, it [liberty] is perversely interpreted both by those who allege it as an excuse for their desires that they may abuse

God's good gifts to their own lust and by those who think that freedom does not exist unless it is used before men, and consequently,
in using it have no regard for weaker brethren.   III, xix, 9

Nothing is plainer than this rule: that we should use our freedom if it results in the edification of our neighbor, but if it does
not help our neighbor, then we should forgo it.   III, xix, 12

LORD'S SUPPER, A REPRESENTATION
And, indeed, we must carefully observe that the very powerful
and almost entire force of the Sacrament lies in these words: "which
is given for you," "which is shed for you." The present distribution
of the body and blood of the Lord would not greatly benefit us
unless they had once for all been given for our redemption and
salvation. They are therefore represented under bread and wine so
that we may learn not only that they are ours but that they have
been destined as food for our spiritual life. And so as we previously
stated, from the physical things set forth in the Sacrament we are
led by a sort of analogy to spiritual things.   IV, xvii, 3

LORD'S SUPPER, ADMINISTRATION OF THE
But as for the outward ceremony of the action—whether or not
the believers take it in their hands, or divide it among themselves, or
severally eat what has been given to each; whether they hand the
cup back to the deacon or give it to the next person; whether the
bread is leavened or unleavened; the wine red or white—it makes
no difference. These things are indifferent, and left at the church's
discretion. . . . Now, to get rid of this great pile of ceremonies,
the Supper could have been administered most becomingly if it
were set before the church very often, and at least once a week.
First, then, it should begin with public prayers. After this a sermon
should be given. Then, when bread and wine have been placed on
the Table, the minister should repeat the words of institution of
the Supper. Next, he should recite the promises which were left to
us in it; at the same time, he should excommunicate all who are
debarred from it by the Lord's prohibition. Afterward, he should

pray that the Lord, with the kindness wherewith he has bestowed this sacred food upon us, also teach and form us to receive it with faith and thankfulness of heart, and, inasmuch as we are not so of ourselves, by his mercy make us worthy of such a feast. But here either psalms should be sung, or something be read, and in becoming order the believers should partake of the most holy banquet, the ministers breaking the bread and giving the cup. When the Supper is finished, there should be an exhortation to sincere faith and confession of faith, to love and behavior worthy of Christians. At the last, thanks should be given, and praises sung to God. When these things are ended, the church should be dismissed in peace.

IV, XVII, 43

LORD'S SUPPER, CHARITY AND THE

We shall benefit very much from the Sacrament if this thought is impressed and engraved upon our minds: that none of the brethren can be injured, despised, rejected, abused, or in any way offended by us, without at the same time, injuring, despising, and abusing Christ by the wrongs we do; that we cannot disagree with our brethren without at the same time disagreeing with Christ; that we cannot love Christ without loving him in the brethren; that we ought to take the same care of our brethren's bodies as we take of our own; for they are members of our body; and that, as no part of our body is touched by any feeling of pain which is not spread among all the rest, so we ought not to allow a brother to be affected by any evil, without being touched with compassion for him. Accordingly, Augustine with good reason frequently calls this Sacrament "the bond of love."   IV, XVII, 38

LORD'S SUPPER, CHRIST AND THE

But greatly mistaken are those who conceive no presence of flesh in the Supper unless it lies in the bread. For thus they leave nothing to the secret working of the Spirit, which unites Christ himself to us. To them Christ does not seem present unless he comes down to us. As though, if he should lift us to himself, we should not just as much enjoy his presence! The question is therefore only of the manner, for they place Christ in the bread, while we do not think it lawful for us to drag him from heaven. Let our readers decide which one is more correct.   IV, xvii, 31

LORD'S SUPPER, HOLY SPIRIT AND THE
Even though it seems unbelievable that Christ's flesh, separated from us by such great distance, penetrates to us, so that it becomes our food, let us remember how far the secret power of the Holy Spirit towers above all our senses, and how foolish it is to wish to measure his immeasurableness by our measure. What, then, our mind does not comprehend, let faith conceive: that the Spirit truly unites things separated in space.   IV, xvii, 10

LORD'S SUPPER, MANNER OF THE
Now, if anyone should ask me how this takes place, I shall not be ashamed to confess that it is a secret too lofty for either my mind to comprehend or my words to declare. And, to speak more plainly, I rather experience than understand it.   IV, xvii, 32

LORD'S SUPPER, MYSTERY OF THE
And although my mind can think beyond what my tongue can utter, yet even my mind is conquered and overwhelmed by the greatness of the thing. Therefore, nothing remains but to break forth in wonder at this mystery, which plainly neither the mind is able to conceive nor the tongue to express.   IV, xvii, 7

LORD'S SUPPER, PARTS OF THE
I therefore say (what has always been accepted in the church and is today taught by all of sound opinion) that the sacred mystery of the Supper consists in two things: physical signs, which, thrust before our eyes, represent to us, according to our feeble capacity, things invisible; and spiritual truth, which is at the same time represented and displayed through the symbols themselves.

IV, xvii, 11

LORD'S SUPPER, SIMPLICITY OF THE

Under the apostles the Lord's Supper was administered with great simplicity. Their immediate successors added something to enhance the dignity of the mystery which was not to be condemned. But afterward they were replaced by those foolish imitators, who, by patching pieces from time to time, contrived for us these priestly vestments that we see in the Mass, these altar ornaments, these gesticulations, and the whole apparatus of useless things.

IV, x, 19

LOVE

But I say: we ought to embrace the whole human race without exception in a single feeling of love; here there is no distinction between barbarian and Greek, worthy and unworthy, friend and enemy, since all should be contemplated in God, not in themselves. When we turn aside from such contemplation, it is no wonder we become entangled in many errors. Therefore, if we rightly direct our love, we must first turn our eyes not to man, the sight of whom would more often engender hate than love, but to God, who bids us extend to all men the love we bear to him, that this may be an unchanging principle: whatever the character of the man, we must yet love him because we love God.   II, viii, 55

MAN, ASPIRATION OF

Here, then, is the course that we must follow if we are to avoid crashing upon these rocks: when man has been taught that no good thing remains in his power, and that he is hedged about on all sides by most miserable necessity, in spite of this he should nevertheless be instructed to aspire to a good of which he is empty, to a freedom of which he has been deprived. In fact, he may thus be more sharply aroused from inactivity than if it were supposed that he was endowed with the highest virtues. II, ii, 1

MAN, DIVINITY OF

Manifold indeed is the nimbleness of the soul with which it surveys heaven and earth, joins past to future, retains in memory something heard long before, nay, pictures to itself whatever it pleases. Manifold also is the skill with which it devises things incredible, and which is the mother of so many marvelous devices. These are unfailing signs of divinity in man.   I, v, 5

MAN, FALL OF

There is no doubt that Adam, when he fell from his state, was by this defection alienated from God. Therefore, even though we grant that God's image was not totally annihilated and destroyed in him, yet it was so corrupted that whatever remains is frightful deformity. Consequently, the beginning of our recovery of salvation is in that restoration which we obtain through Christ, who also is called the Second Adam for the reason that he restores us to true and complete integrity.   I, xv, 4

But Paul, calling Christ the "Second Adam," sets the Fall, from which arose the necessity of restoring nature to its former condition, between man's first origin and the restoration that we obtain through Christ. It follows, then, that it was for this same cause that the Son of God was born to become man.   II, xii, 7

The decree [Fall of Adam] is dreadful indeed, I confess. Yet no one can deny that God foreknew what end man was to have before he created him, and consequently foreknew because he so ordained by his decree.   III, xxiii, 7

Accordingly, man falls according as God's providence ordains, but he falls by his own fault.   III, xxiii, 8

MAN, FREEDOM OF

Therefore Adam could have stood if he wished, seeing that he fell solely by his own will. But it was because his will was capable of being bent to one side or the other, and was not given the constancy to persevere, that he fell so easily. Yet his choice of good and evil was free. . . .   I, xv, 8

MAN, NATURAL

Hence we can see how uneasy in mind all those persons are who order their lives according to their own plan. We can see how artfully they strive—to the point of weariness—to obtain the goal of their ambition or avarice, while, on the other hand, avoiding poverty and a lowly condition.   III, vii, 8

MAN, ORIGINAL NATURE OF

Now we need bear only this in mind: man was far different at the first creation from his whole posterity, who, deriving their origin from him in his corrupted state, have contracted from him a hereditary taint. For, the individual parts of his soul were formed to uprightness, the soundness of his mind stood firm, and his will was free to choose the good. If anyone objects that his will was placed in an insecure position because its power was weak, his status should have availed to remove any excuse; nor was it reasonable for God to be constrained by the necessity of making a man who either could not or would not sin at all. Such a nature would, indeed, have been more excellent. But to quarrel with God on this precise point, as if he ought to have conferred this upon man, is more than iniquitous, inasmuch as it was in his own choice to give whatever he pleased. But the reason he did not sustain man by the virtue of perseverance lies hidden in his plan; sobriety is for us the part of wisdom. Man, indeed, received the ability provided he exercised the will; but he did not have the will to use his ability, for this exercising of the will would have been followed by perseverance. Yet he is not excusable, for he received so much that he voluntarily brought about his own destruction; indeed, no necessity was imposed upon God of giving man other than a mediocre and even transitory will, that from man's Fall he might gather occasion for his own glory.   I, xv, 8

MAN, POVERTY OF

Nevertheless, what I mentioned at the beginning of this chapter I am compelled here to repeat once more: that whoever is utterly cast down and overwhelmed by the awareness of his calamity, poverty, nakedness, and disgrace has thus advanced farthest in knowledge of himself. For there is no danger of man's depriving himself of too much so long as he learns that in God must be recouped what he himself lacks.   II, ii, 10

MAN, PRIDE OF (see GOD, LOVE OF)

MAN, STRENGTH OF

When we are taught to wage our own war, we are but borne aloft on a reed stick, only to fall as soon as it breaks! Yet we flatter our strength unduly when we compare it even to a reed stick! For whatever vain men devise and babble concerning these matters is but smoke.   II, ii, 1

MANICHAEANS AND MARCIONITES

Indeed, the genuineness of his [Christ's] human nature was impugned long ago by both the Manichees and the Marcionites. The Marcionites fancied Christ's body a mere appearance, while the Manichees dreamed that he was endowed with heavenly flesh. But many strong testimonies of Scripture stand against both.

II, xiii, 1

MARRIAGE

Therefore let not married persons think that all things are permitted to them, but let each man have his own wife soberly, and each wife her own husband. So doing, let them not admit anything at all that is unworthy of the honorableness and temperance of marriage.   II, viii, 44

MASS

The Lord often testifies that he recognizes no righteousness of works except in the perfect observance of his law. What perversity is it for us, when we lack righteousness, in order not to seem deprived of all glory—that is, utterly to have yielded to God—to boast of some little bits of a few works and try through other satisfactions to pay for what is lacking? Satisfactions have already been effectively demolished, so that they ought not even to come to our minds in a dream. I say that those who talk such nonsense do not realize what an execrable thing sin is in God's sight. Truly, they should have understood that men's whole righteousness, gathered together in one heap, could not make compensation for a single sin.   III, xiv, 13

If Christ is sacrificed in each and every Mass, he must be cruelly slain in a thousand places at every moment.   IV, xviii, 5

What remains but that the blind may see, the deaf hear, and even children understand this abomination of the Mass? Offered in a golden cup, it has so inebriated all kings and peoples of the earth, from highest to lowest, and has so stricken them with drowsiness and dizziness, that, more stupid than brute beasts, they have steered the whole vessel of their salvation into this one deadly whirlpool. Surely, Satan never prepared a stronger engine to besiege and capture Christ's Kingdom. This is the Helen for whom the enemies of truth today do battle with so much rage, fury, and cruelty—a Helen indeed, with whom they so defile themselves in spiritual fornication, the most abominable of all.   IV, xviii, 18

MEDIATOR, DEATH OF THE
The Spirit usually speaks in this way in the Scriptures: "God was men's enemy until they were reconciled to grace by the death of Christ." "They were under a curse until their iniquity was atoned for by his sacrifice." "They were estranged from God until through his body they were reconciled." Expressions of this sort have been accommodated to our capacity that we may better understand how miserable and ruinous our condition is apart from Christ.
                                                                II, xvi, 2

MEDIATOR, EXAMPLE OF THE
From this also arises the comfort for our anguish and sorrow that the apostle holds out to us: that this Mediator has experienced our weaknesses the better to succor us in our miseries.   II, xvi, 12

MEDIATOR, GRACE OF THE

This will become even clearer if we call to mind that what the Mediator was to accomplish was no common thing. His task was so to restore us to God's grace as to make of the children of men, children of God; of the heirs of Gehenna, heirs of the Heavenly Kingdom. Who could have done this had not the selfsame Son of God become the Son of man, and had not so taken what was ours as to impart what was his to us, and to make what was his by nature ours by grace? . . . It was his task to swallow up death. Who but the Life could do this?   II, xii, 2

MEDIATOR, NECESSITY OF THE

Hence, it was necessary for the Son of God to become for us "Immanuel, that is, God with us," and in such a way that his divinity and our human nature might by mutual connection grow together. Otherwise the nearness would not have been near enough, nor the affinity sufficiently firm, for us to hope that God might dwell with us.   II, xii, 1

MEDIATOR, WORK OF THE

We see that our whole salvation and all its parts are comprehended in Christ. We should therefore take care not to derive the least portion of it from anywhere else. If we seek salvation, we are taught by the very name of Jesus that it is "of him." If we seek any other gifts of the Spirit, they will be found in his anointing. If we seek strength, it lies in his dominion; if purity, in his conception; if gentleness, it appears in his birth. For by his birth he was made like us in all respects that he might learn to feel our pain. If we seek redemption, it lies in his passion; if acquittal, in his condemnation; if remission of the curse, in his cross; if satisfaction, in his sacrifice; if purification, in his blood; if reconciliation, in his descent into hell; if mortification of the flesh, in his tomb; if newness of life, in his resurrection; if immortality, in the same; if inheritance of the Heavenly Kingdom, in his entrance into heaven; if protection, if security, if abundant supply of all blessings, in his Kingdom; if untroubled expectation of judgment, in the power given to him to judge. In short, since rich store of every kind of good abounds in him, let us drink our fill from this fountain, and from no other. Some men, not content with him alone, are borne hither and thither from one hope to another; even if they concern themselves chiefly with him, they nevertheless stray from the right way in turning some part of their thinking in another direction. Yet such distrust cannot creep in where men have once for all truly known the abundance of his blessings.   II, xvi, 19

MEDITATION

But believers know by use and experience that ardor burns low unless they supply new fuel. Accordingly, among our prayers, meditation both on God's nature and on his Word is by no means superfluous.   III, xx, 13

MEEKNESS

You will never attain true gentleness except by one path: a heart imbued with lowliness and with reverence for others.   III, vii, 4

MINISTRY, BISHOPS AND PRESBYTERS

All those to whom the office of teaching was enjoined they called "presbyters." In each city these chose one of their number to whom they specially gave the title "bishop" in order that dissensions might not arise (as commonly happens) from equality of rank. Still, the bishop was not so much higher in honor and dignity as to have lordship over his colleagues. But the same functions that the consul has in the senate—to report on business, to request opinions, to preside over others in counseling, admonishing, and exhorting, to govern the whole action by his authority, and to carry out what was decreed by common decision—the bishop carried out in the assembly of presbyters. And the ancients themselves admit that this was introduced by human agreement to meet the need of the times. Thus Jerome, commenting on the letter to Titus, says: "Bishop and presbyter are one and the same."   IV, iv, 2

MINISTRY, CALL TO THE

Therefore, in order that noisy and troublesome men should not rashly take upon themselves to teach or to rule (which might otherwise happen), especial care was taken that no one should assume public office in the church without being called. Therefore, if a man were to be considered a true minister of the church, he must first have been duly called, then he must respond to his calling, that is, he must undertake and carry out the tasks enjoined.   IV, III, 10

I am speaking of the outward and solemn call which has to do with the public order of the church. I pass over that secret call, of which each minister is conscious before God, and which does not have the church as witness. But there is the good witness of our heart that we receive the proffered office not with ambition or avarice, not with any other selfish desire, but with a sincere fear of God and desire to build up the church.   IV, III, 11

MINISTRY, DISCIPLINE OF THE

There follows the second part of discipline, which applies particularly to the clergy. It is contained in the canons that the ancient bishops imposed upon themselves and their order. Such are these: no cleric should devote himself to hunting, gambling, or reveling. No cleric should practice usury or commerce; no cleric should be present at wanton dances—and there are others of this sort.

IV, XII, 22

MINISTRY, MARRIAGE AND THE

Surely the forbidding of marriage to priests came about by an impious tyranny not only against God's Word but also against all equity. First, to forbid what the Lord left free was by no means lawful to men. Again, that the Lord expressly took care by his Word that this freedom should not be infringed upon is too clear to require a long proof. I pass over the fact that Paul in many passages wishes a bishop to be a man of one wife. But what could be more forcefully said than when he declares by the Holy Spirit that in the Last Days there will be impious men who forbid marriage, and calls them not only impostors but demons?   IV, XII, 23

But if my adversaries claim antiquity against me, my first answer is that this freedom of bishops to be married existed both under the apostles and for some centuries afterward. The apostles themselves, and those pastors of prime authority who followed in their place, used this freedom without any difficulty.   IV, xii, 27

MINISTRY, OBEDIENCE IN THE

This is also a prime requisite for the moderation of discipline, as Augustine argues against the Donatists: that individual laymen, if they see vices not diligently enough corrected by the council of elders, should not therefore at once depart from the church; and that the pastors themselves, if they cannot cleanse all that needs correction according to their hearts' desire, should not for that reason resign their ministry or disturb the entire church with un-accustomed rigor. For what Augustine writes is very true: "Who-ever either corrects what he can by reproof, or excludes, without breaking the bond of peace, what he cannot correct—disapproving with fairness, bearing with firmness—this man is free and loosed from the curse."   IV, xii, 11

MINISTRY, TEACHERS AND THE

Next come pastors and teachers, whom the church can never go without. There is, I believe, this difference between them: teachers are not put in charge of discipline, or administering the sacraments, or warnings and exhortations, but only of Scriptural interpretation —to keep doctrine whole and pure among believers. But the pastoral office includes all these functions within itself.   IV, iii, 4

MINISTRY, WOMEN AND THE

The practice before Augustine was born is first of all inferred from Tertullian, who held that a woman was not allowed to speak in the church, and also not to teach, to baptize, or to offer. This was that she might not claim for herself the function of any man, much less that of a priest. Epiphanius also is a trustworthy witness of this matter when he upbraids Marcion for having given women permission to baptize. And I am well aware of the answer of those who think otherwise: that there is a great difference between common usage and an extraordinary remedy required by dire necessity. But since Epiphanius declares that it is a mockery to give women the right to baptize and makes no exception, it is clear enough that he condemns this corrupt practice as inexcusable under any pretext. Also in the third book, where he teaches that permission was not even given to the holy mother of Christ, he adds no reservation.

IV, xv, 21

MINISTRY, WORK OF

And in order that the preaching of the gospel might flourish, he [God] deposited this treasure in the church. He instituted "pastors and teachers" through whose lips he might teach his own; he furnished them with authority; finally, he omitted nothing that might make for holy agreement of faith and for right order.   IV, i, 1

There are, then, two passages which speak of binding and loosing. One is Matt., ch. 16, where Christ, after promising to give the keys of the Kingdom of Heaven to Peter, immediately adds that whatever he binds or looses on earth shall be confirmed in heaven. By these words he means the same thing as by the other words which occur in John, when, about to send the disciples out to preach, after he breathes on them, he says, "If you forgive the sins of any, they will be forgiven; if you retain the sins of any, they will be retained in heaven." I shall bring to this an interpretation not subtle, not forced, not distorted; but natural, fluent, and plain. This command concerning forgiving and retaining sins and that promise made to Peter concerning binding and loosing ought to be referred solely to the ministry of the Word, because when the Lord committed his ministry to the apostles, he also equipped them for the office of binding and loosing. For what is the sum total of the gospel except that we all, being slaves of sin and death, are released and freed through the redemption which is in Christ Jesus? and that they who do not receive or acknowledge Christ as their liberator and redeemer are condemned and sentenced to eternal chains? . . . We conclude that in those passages the power of the keys is simply the preaching of the gospel, and that with regard to men it is not so much power as ministry. For Christ has not given this power actually to men, but to his Word, of which he has made men ministers.   IV, xi, 1

The remaining part of discipline, which is not properly contained within the power of the keys, is where the pastors, according to the need of the times, should exhort the people either to fasting or to solemn supplications, or to other acts of humility, repentance, and faith—of which the time, the manner, and the form are not prescribed by God's Word, but left to the judgment of the church.

IV, xii, 14

MIRACLE
How plainly and clearly is his deity shown in miracles! Even though I confess that both the prophets and the apostles performed miracles equal to and similar to his, yet in this respect there is the greatest of differences: they distributed the gifts of God by their ministry, but he showed forth his own power.   I, xiii, 13

MIRROR, ANGELS A
Likewise, on this account they [angels] are more than once called gods, because in their ministry as in a mirror they in some respect exhibit his divinity to us.   I, xiv, 5

MIRROR, CHRIST THE
Accordingly, those whom God has adopted as his sons are said to have been chosen not in themselves but in his Christ; for unless he could love them in him, he could not honor them with the inheritance of his Kingdom if they had not previously become partakers of him. But if we have been chosen in him, we shall not find assurance of our election in ourselves; and not even in God the Father, if we conceive him as severed from his Son. Christ, then, is the mirror wherein we must, and without self-deception may, contemplate our own election. For since it is into his body the Father

has destined those to be engrafted whom he has willed from eternity to be his own, that he may hold as sons all whom he acknowledges to be among his members, we have a sufficiently clear and firm testimony that we have been inscribed in the book of life.

III, xxiv, 5

MIRROR, CREATURES A

There is no doubt that the Lord would have us uninterruptedly occupied in this holy meditation; that, while we contemplate in all creatures, as in mirrors, those immense riches of his wisdom, justice, goodness, and power, we should not merely run over them cursorily, and, so to speak, with a fleeting glance; but we should ponder them at length, turn them over in our minds seriously and faithfully, and recollect them repeatedly.   I, xiv, 21

MIRROR, THE DEPARTED AS A

Our adversaries, indeed, babble in their own shadows something or other about the radiance of God's face shining upon the saints, in which, as in a mirror, they may gaze upon the affairs of men from on high. Yet what is it to affirm this, especially with such boldness as they dare to do, but to wish through a drunken dream of our brain to break into and penetrate God's secret judgments apart from his Word, and to trample upon Scripture?   III, xx, 24

MIRROR, DOCTRINE A

We must observe that God always revealed himself thus to the holy patriarchs in the mirror of his teaching in order to be known spiritually.   IV, i, 5

MIRROR, HEBREW PEOPLE A

We contend, on the contrary, that, in the earthly possession they [the Hebrew people] enjoyed, they looked, as in a mirror, upon the future inheritance they believed to have been prepared for them in heaven.   II, xi, 1

From this it follows that both among the whole tribe of Levi and among the posterity of David, Christ was set before the eyes of the ancient folk as in a double mirror.   II, vii, 2

MIRROR, HUMAN RACE A
A clear mirror of God's works is in humankind.   I, v, 3

MIRROR, LAW A (see LAW, A MIRROR)

MIRROR, MAN A
So man was created in the image of God; in him the Creator himself willed that his own glory be seen as in a mirror.   II, xii, 6

MIRROR, MOSES A
In brief, Moses' one song is a bright mirror in which God is manifest.   I, viii, 7

In short, let us remember that that invisible God, whose wisdom, power, and righteousness are incomprehensible, sets before us Moses' history as a mirror in which his living likeness glows.

I, xiv, 1

MIRROR, RESURRECTION A
He [Christ] was raised by the power of the Holy Spirit, the Quickener of us in common with him. Finally, he was raised that he might be "the resurrection and the life." As we have said that in this mirror the living image of the resurrection is visible to us, so is it a firm foundation to support our minds, provided we are not wearied or irked with a longer delay; for our task is not to measure minutes of time as we please but patiently to wait until God in his own good time restores his Kingdom.   III, xxv, 3

MIRROR, SACRAMENTS A

Here our merciful Lord, according to his infinite kindness, so tempers himself to our capacity that, since we are creatures who always creep on the ground, cleave to the flesh, and do not think about or even conceive of anything spiritual, he condescends to lead us to himself even by these earthly elements, and to set before us in the flesh a mirror of spiritual blessings.   IV, xiv, 3

Or we might call them [sacraments] mirrors in which we may contemplate the riches of God's grace, which he lavishes upon us. For by them he manifests himself to us (as has already been said) as far as our dullness is given to perceive, and attests his good will and love toward us more expressly than by word.   IV, xiv, 6

MIRROR, SOUL A

For that speculation of Augustine, that the soul is the reflection (mirror) of the Trinity because in it reside the understanding, will, and memory, is by no means sound.   I, xv, 4

MIRROR, UNIVERSE A

This skillful ordering of the universe is for us a sort of mirror in which we can contemplate God, who is otherwise invisible.

I, v, 1

MIRROR, WORD A

Therefore, take away the Word and no faith will then remain. We are not here discussing whether a human ministry is necessary for the sowing of God's Word, from which faith may be conceived. This we shall discuss in another place. But we say that the Word itself, however it be imparted to us, is like a mirror in which faith may contemplate God.   III, ii, 6

MIRROR, WORKS A (see GOD, WORKS OF)

MODERATION
But since he [Christ] was uncorrupted, a moderation that restrained excess flourished in all his emotions. Hence, he could be like us in sorrow, fear, and dread, yet in such a way as to differ from us by this characteristic.   II, xvi, 12

MORALITY
Duties are weighed not by deeds but by ends.   III, xiv, 3

MURDER
He who has merely refrained from shedding blood has not therefore avoided the crime of murder. If you perpetrate anything by deed, if you plot anything by attempt, if you wish or plan anything contrary to the safety of a neighbor, you are considered guilty of murder. Again, unless you endeavor to look out for his safety according to your ability and opportunity, you are violating the law with a like heinousness.

Scripture notes that this commandment rests upon a twofold basis: man is both the image of God, and our flesh.   II, viii, 40

NATURE
Yet hence it appears that if men were taught only by nature, they would hold to nothing certain or solid or clear-cut, but would be so tied to confused principles as to worship an unknown god.

I, v, 12

Meanwhile let us not be ashamed to take pious delight in the works of God open and manifest in this most beautiful theater.

I, xiv, 20

Indeed, as I pointed out a little before, God himself has shown by the order of Creation that he created all things for man's sake.

I, xiv, 22

OATH

In the first place, we must state what an oath is. It is calling God as witness to confirm the truth of our word.   II, VIII, 23

If we understand this, we will not think that Christ condemned oaths entirely, but only those which transgress the rule of the law.

II, VIII, 26

For if it is lawful in a grave and serious matter for private persons to call upon God as a judge between them, there is even greater reason to call upon him as a witness. Your brother will accuse you of breach of faith; as a duty of love you will try to clear yourself. On no terms will he admit himself satisfied. If your reputation is imperiled because of his stubborn ill will, you can without offense call upon God's judgment to make manifest your innocence in due time. . . . Thus I have no better rule than for us so to control our oaths that they may serve a just need—either to vindicate the Lord's glory, or to further a brother's edification. Such is the purpose of this commandment of the law.   II, VIII, 27

OBEDIENCE

These detractors are, moreover, deceived in this one point: they do not recognize in Christ a weakness pure and free of all vice and stain because he held himself within the bounds of obedience.

II, XVI, 12

PATIENCE

Suppose, however, the whisperings of the malevolent so fill your ears that the accused have no chance to speak for themselves, but those savage furies, while you connive at them, ever rage against us with imprisonings, scourgings, rackings, maimings, and burnings. Then we will be reduced to the last extremity even as sheep destined for the slaughter. Yet this will so happen that "in our patience we may possess our souls"; and may await the strong hand of the Lord, which will surely appear in due season, coming forth armed to deliver the poor from their affliction and also to punish their despisers, who now exult with such great assurance.

DEDICATION

I decided to say this in order to recall godly minds from despair, lest, because they cannot cast off the natural feeling of sorrow, they forthwith renounce the pursuit of patience. This must necessarily happen to those who make patience into insensibility, and a valiant and constant man into a stock. For Scripture praises the saints for their forbearance when, so afflicted with harsh misfortune, they do not break or fall; so stabbed with bitterness, they are at the same time flooded with spiritual joy; so pressed by apprehension, they recover their breath, revived by God's consolation.   III, VIII, 10

From this point he [Augustine] concludes with Cyprian: "Let a man mercifully correct what he can; let him patiently bear what he cannot correct, and groan and sorrow over it with love."

IV, XII, 11

PEACE

And I have not forgotten what I have previously said, the memory of which is repeatedly renewed by experience: faith is tossed about by various doubts, so that the minds of the godly are rarely at peace —at least they do not always enjoy a peaceful state. But whatever siege engines may shake them, they either rise up out of the very gulf of temptations, or stand fast upon their watch. Indeed, this assurance alone nourishes and protects faith—when we hold fast to what is said in the psalm: "The Lord is our protection, our help in tribulation. Therefore we will not fear while the earth shakes, and the mountains leap into the heart of the sea." Another psalm, also, extols this very sweet repose: "I lay down and slept; I awoke again, for the Lord sustained me." Not that David always dwelt in a tranquil and happy state! But to the extent that he tasted God's grace, according to the measure of faith, he boasts that he fearlessly despises everything that could trouble his peace of mind.

III, II, 37

Now if we ask in what way the conscience can be made quiet before God, we shall find the only way to be that unmerited righteousness be conferred upon us as a gift of God.   III, XIII, 3

PERFECTION

For since no perfection can come to us so long as we are clothed in this flesh, and the law moreover announces death and judgment to all who do not maintain perfect righteousness in works, it will always have grounds for accusing and condemning us unless, on the contrary, God's mercy counters it, and by continual forgiveness of sins repeatedly acquits us.   III, XIV, 10

PERSEVERANCE

There is no other reason why some persevere to the end, while others fall at the beginning of the course. For perseverance itself is indeed also a gift of God, which he does not bestow on all indiscriminately, but imparts to whom he pleases.   II, v, 3

Only his elect does he [God] account worthy of receiving the living root of faith so that they may endure to the end.   III, II, 11

Therefore, we repeat what we have already stated: that the root of faith can never be torn from the godly breast, but clings so fast to the inmost parts that, however faith seems to be shaken or to bend this way or that, its light is never so extinguished or snuffed out that it does not at least lurk as it were beneath the ashes. And this example shows that the Word, which is an incorruptible seed, brings forth fruit like itself, whose fertility never wholly dries up and dies.   III, II, 21

PIETY

I call "piety" that reverence joined with love of God which the knowledge of his benefits induces. For until men recognize that they owe everything to God, that they are nourished by his fatherly care, that he is the Author of their every good, that they should seek nothing beyond him—they will never yield him willing service. Nay, unless they establish their complete happiness in him, they will never give themselves truly and sincerely to him.   I, ii, 1

And so, lest they should everywhere seem to despise him whose majesty weighs upon them, they perform some semblance of religion. Meanwhile they do not desist from polluting themselves with every sort of vice, and from joining wickedness to wickedness, until in every respect they violate the holy law of the Lord and dissipate all his righteousness. Or at least they are not so restrained by that pretended fear of God from wallowing blithely in their own sins and flattering themselves, and preferring to indulge their fleshly intemperance rather than restrain it by the bridle of the Holy Spirit. This, however, is but a vain and false shadow of religion, scarcely even worth being called a shadow. From it one may easily grasp anew how much this confused knowledge of God differs from the piety from which religion takes its source, which is instilled in the breasts of believers only.   I, iv, 4

Only let the readers agree on this point: let the first step toward godliness be to recognize that God is our Father to watch over us, govern and nourish us, until he gather us unto the eternal inheritance of his Kingdom.   II, vi, 4

. . . let us comfort ourselves with the thought that we are rendering that obedience which the Lord requires when we suffer anything rather than turn aside from piety.   IV, xx, 32

PLATO

Plato, on seeing men's want of skill in making requests to God, which, if granted, would often have been disadvantageous to them, declares this, taken from an ancient poet, to be the best prayer: "King Jupiter, bestow the best things upon us whether we wish for them or not, but command that evil things be far from us even when we request them." And, indeed, the heathen man is wise in that he judges how dangerous it is to seek from the Lord what our greed dictates; at the same time he discloses our unhappiness, in that we cannot even open our mouths before God without danger unless the Spirit instructs us in the right pattern for prayer.   III, xx, 34

PLEASURE

Now if we ponder to what end God created food, we shall find that he meant not only to provide for necessity but also for delight and good cheer. Thus the purpose of clothing, apart from necessity, was comeliness and decency. In grasses, trees, and fruits, apart from their various uses, there is beauty of appearance and pleasantness of odor. For if this were not true, the prophet would not have reckoned them among the benefits of God, "that wine gladdens the heart of man, that oil makes his face shine." Scripture would not have reminded us repeatedly, in commending his kindness, that he gave all such things to men.   III, x, 2

Away, then, with that inhuman philosophy which, while conceding only a necessary use of creatures, not only malignantly deprives us of the lawful fruit of God's beneficence but cannot be practiced unless it robs a man of all his senses and degrades him to a block. But no less diligently, on the other hand, we must resist the lust of the flesh, which, unless it is kept in order, overflows without measure. And it has, as I have said, its own advocates, who, under the pretext of the freedom conceded, permit everything to it. First, one bridle is put upon it if it be determined that all things were created for us that we might recognize the Author and give thanks for his kindness toward us. . . . For many so enslave all their senses to delights that the mind lies overwhelmed. Many are so delighted with marble, gold, and pictures that they become marble, they turn, as it were, into metals and are like painted figures. The smell of the kitchen or the sweetness of its odors so stupefies others that they are unable to smell anything spiritual.   III, x, 3

POMP

So today not only the untutored crowd but any man who is greatly puffed up with worldly wisdom is marvelously captivated by ceremonial pomp.   IV, x, 12

PRAISE

Show me a man, if you can, who, unless he has according to the commandment of the Lord renounced himself, would freely exercise goodness among men. For all who have not been possessed with this feeling have at least followed virtue for the sake of praise.

III, vii, 2

PRAYER, ANSWER TO

But if finally even after long waiting our senses cannot learn the benefit received from prayer, or perceive any fruit from it, still our faith will make us sure of what cannot be perceived by sense, that we have obtained what was expedient. For the Lord so often and so certainly promises to care for us in our troubles, when they have once been laid upon his bosom. And so he will cause us to possess abundance in poverty, and comfort in affliction.   III, xx, 52

PRAYER, BELIEF IN

It is amazing how much our lack of trust provokes God if we request of him a boon that we do not expect. . . . To sum up, it is faith that obtains whatever is granted to prayer.   III, xx, 11

PRAYER, CHRIST AND

For as soon as God's dread majesty comes to mind, we cannot but tremble and be driven far away by the recognition of our own unworthiness, until Christ comes forward as intermediary, to change the throne of dreadful glory into the throne of grace. As the apostle also teaches how we should dare with all confidence to appear, to receive mercy, and to find grace in timely help.   III, xx, 17

Now even as we have taught that by Christ's intercession are consecrated our prayers, which would otherwise have been unclean, so the apostle, enjoining us to offer a sacrifice of praise through Christ, warns us that our mouths are not clean enough to sing the praises of God's name until Christ's priesthood intercedes for us.

III, xx, 28

PRAYER, DESIGN OF
From this, moreover, it is fully evident that unless voice and song, if interposed in prayer, spring from deep feeling of heart, neither has any value or profit in the least with God. . . . But the chief use of the tongue is in public prayers, which are offered in the assembly of believers, by which it comes about that with one common voice, and as it were, with the same mouth, we all glorify God together, worshipping him with one spirit and the same faith. And we do this openly, that all men mutually, each one from his brother, may receive the confession of faith and be invited and prompted by his example.   III, xx, 31

PRAYER, DIVINE MERCY IN
But God tolerates even our stammering and pardons our ignorance whenever something inadvertently escapes us; as indeed without this mercy there would be no freedom to pray.   III, xx, 16

PRAYER, END OF
Surely, with good reason the Heavenly Father affirms that the only stronghold of safety is in calling upon his name. By so doing we invoke the presence both of his providence, through which he watches over and guards our affairs, and of his power, through which he sustains us, weak as we are and well-nigh overcome, and of his goodness, through which he receives us, miserably burdened with sins, unto grace; and, in short, it is by prayer that we call him to reveal himself as wholly present to us.   III, xx, 2

PRAYER, GIFT OF
The godly man enjoys a pure conscience before the Lord, thus confirming himself in the promises with which the Lord comforts and supports his true worshipers. It is not our intent to snatch this blessing from his breast; rather, we would assert that his assurance his prayers will be answered rests solely upon God's clemency, apart from all consideration of personal merit.   III, xx, 10

PRAYER, HOLY SPIRIT AND

As we must turn keenness of mind toward God, so affection of heart has to follow. Both, indeed, stand far beneath; nay, more truly, they faint and fail, or are carried in the opposite direction. Therefore, in order to minister to this weakness, God gives us the Spirit as our teacher in prayer, to tell us what is right and temper our emotions.   III, xx, 5

PRAYER, INWARDNESS OF

Prayer is something secret, which is both principally lodged in the heart and requires a tranquillity far from all our teeming cares.

III, xx, 29

For since we ourselves are God's true temples, if we would call upon God in his holy temple, we must pray within ourselves.

III, xx, 30

PRAYER, METHODS OF

These two matters are well worth attention: first, whoever engages in prayer should apply to it his faculties and efforts, and not, as commonly happens, be distracted by wandering thoughts. . . . We have noted another point: not to ask any more than God allows.

III, xx, 5

PRAYER, OTHERS AND

To sum up, all prayers ought to be such as to look to that community which our Lord has established in his Kingdom and his household. . . . Nevertheless, this does not prevent us from praying especially for ourselves and for certain others, provided, however, our minds do not withdraw their attention from this community or turn aside from it but refer all things to it.   III, xx, 38–39

PRAYER, PERSEVERANCE IN

If, with minds composed to this obedience, we allow ourselves to be ruled by the laws of divine providence, we shall easily learn to persevere in prayer and, with desires suspended, patiently to wait for the Lord. Then we shall be sure that, even though he does not appear, he is always present to us, and will in his own time declare how he has never had ears deaf to the prayers that in men's eyes he seems to have neglected.   III, xx, 51

PRAYER, POINT OF

It is, therefore, by the benefit of prayer that we reach those riches which are laid up for us with the Heavenly Father. For there is a communion of men with God by which, having entered the heavenly sanctuary, they appeal to him in person concerning his promises in order to experience, where necessity so demands, that what they believed was not vain, although he had promised it in word alone.

III, xx, 2

PRAYER, REASON FOR

But, someone will say, does God not know, even without being reminded, both in what respect we are troubled and what is expedient for us, so that it may seem in a sense superfluous that he should be stirred up by our prayers—as if he were drowsily blinking or even sleeping until he is aroused by our voice? But they who thus reason do not observe to what end the Lord instructed his people to pray, for he ordained it not so much for his own sake as for ours. . . . It will be enough for us to note the single example of Elijah, who, sure of God's purpose, after he has deliberately promised rain to King Ahab, still anxiously prays with his head between his knees, and sends his servant seven times to look, not because he would discredit his prophecy, but because he knew it was his duty, lest his faith be sleepy or sluggish, to lay his desires before God. Therefore, even though, while we grow dull and stupid toward our miseries, he watches and keeps guard on our behalf, and sometimes even helps us unasked, still it is very important for us to call upon him: First, that our hearts may be fired with a zealous and burning desire ever to seek, love, and serve him, while we become accustomed in every need to flee to him as to a sacred anchor. Secondly, that there may enter our hearts no desire and no wish at all of which we should be ashamed to make him a witness, while we learn to set all our wishes before his eyes, and even to pour out our whole hearts. Thirdly, that we be prepared to receive his benefits with true gratitude of heart and thanksgiving, benefits that our prayer reminds us come from his hand. Fourthly, moreover, that, having obtained what we were seeking, and being convinced that he has answered our prayers, we should be led to meditate upon his kindness more ardently. And fifthly, that at the same time we embrace with greater delight those things which we acknowledge to have been obtained by prayers. Finally, that use and experience may, according to the measure of our feebleness, confirm his providence, while we understand not only that he promises never to fail us, and of his own will opens the way to call upon him at the very point of necessity, but also that he ever extends his hand to help his own, not wet-nursing them with words but defending them with present help.   III, xx, 3

PRAYER, THE LORD'S

In so teaching, we mean only this: that no man should ask for, expect, or demand, anything at all except what is included, by way of summary, in this prayer; and though the words may be utterly different, yet the sense ought not to vary.   III, xx, 49

PRAYER, TIME OF

Now if we should consider how many dangers at every moment threaten, fear itself will teach us that we at no single time may leave off praying.   III, xx, 7

But, although it has already been stated above that, lifting up our hearts, we should ever aspire to God and pray without ceasing, still, since our weakness is such that it has to be supported by many aids, and our sluggishness such that it needs to be goaded, it is fitting each one of us should set apart certain hours for this exercise.

III, xx, 50

PRAYERS FOR THE DEAD

All reasons of this sort are lacking in the case of the dead; when the Lord withdrew them from our company, he left us no contact with them, and as far as we can conjecture, not even left them any with us.   III, xx, 24

PRAYERS OF SAINTS

Meanwhile, notwithstanding, the saints still retain their intercessions, whereby they commend one another's salvation to God. The apostle mentions these, but all depend solely upon Christ's intercession, so far are they from detracting from his in any way. For as they gush forth from the emotion of love, in which we willingly and freely embrace one another as members of one body, so also are they related to the unity of the Head. When, therefore, those intercessions are also made in Christ's name, what else do they attest but that no one can be helped by any prayers at all save when Christ intercedes? Christ does not by his intercession hinder us from pleading for one another by prayers in the church. So, then, let it remain an established principle that we should direct all intercessions of the whole church to that sole intercession.   III, xx, 19

PREACHING

Many are led either by pride, dislike, or rivalry to the conviction that they can profit enough from private reading and meditation; hence they despise public assemblies and deem preaching superfluous. But, since they do their utmost to sever or break the sacred bond of unity, no one escapes the just penalty of this unholy separation without bewitching himself with pestilent errors and foulest delusions. In order, then, that pure simplicity of faith may flourish among us, let us not be reluctant to use this exercise of religion which God, by ordaining it, has shown us to be necessary and highly approved.   IV, i, 5

PREDESTINATION, CHRIST'S PLACE IN

Indeed, as Augustine very truly writes: "The clearest light of predestination and grace is the Man Christ Jesus, the Savior, who brought this to pass by the human nature that was in him, through no preceding merits of works or of faith. . . . Apart from God's good pleasure Christ could not merit anything; but did so because he had been appointed to appease God's wrath with his sacrifice, and to blot out our transgressions with his obedience. II, xvii, 1

PREDESTINATION, CHRIST'S WORK IN

He alone is well founded in Christ who has perfect righteousness in himself: since the apostle does not say that He was sent to help us attain righteousness but himself to be our righteousness. Indeed, he states "that he has chosen us in him" from eternity "before the foundation of the world," through no merit of our own "but according to the purpose of divine good pleasure." III, xv, 5

PREDESTINATION, ELECTION AND

We shall never be clearly persuaded, as we ought to be, that our salvation flows from the wellspring of God's free mercy until we come to know his eternal election, which illumines God's grace by this contrast: that he does not indiscriminately adopt all into the hope of salvation but gives to some what he denies to others. How much the ignorance of this principle detracts from God's glory, how much it takes away from true humility. III, xxi, 1

PREDESTINATION, END OF

For it is not right for man unrestrainedly to search out things that the Lord has willed to be hid in himself, and to unfold from eternity itself the sublimest wisdom, which he would have us revere but not understand that through this also he should fill us with wonder.

III, xxi, 1

PREDESTINATION, FAITH AND

From this believers have some taste of what we set out at the beginning: predestination, rightly understood, brings no shaking of faith but rather its best confirmation. III, xxiv, 9

PREDESTINATION, FOREKNOWLEDGE AND

No one who wishes to be thought religious dares simply deny predestination, by which God adopts some to hope of life, and sentences others to eternal death. But our opponents, especially those who make foreknowledge its cause, envelop it in numerous petty objections. We, indeed, place both doctrines in God, but we say that subjecting one to the other is absurd. When we attribute foreknowledge to God, we mean that all things always were, and perpetually remain, under his eyes, so that to his knowledge there is nothing future or past, but all things are present. And they are present in such a way that he not only conceives them through ideas, as we have before us those things which our minds remember, but he truly looks upon them and discerns them as things placed before him. And this foreknowledge is extended throughout the universe to every creature. We call predestination God's eternal decree, by which he determined with himself what he willed to become of each man. For all are not created in equal condition; rather, eternal life is foreordained for some, eternal damnation for others. Therefore, as any man has been created to one or the other of these ends, we speak of him as predestined to life or to death.   III, xxi, 5

If God only foresaw human events, and did not also dispose and determine them by his decision, then there would be some point in raising this question: whether his foreseeing had anything to do with their necessity. But since he foresees future events only by reason of the fact that he decreed that they take place, they vainly raise a quarrel over foreknowledge, when it is clear that all things take place rather by his determination and bidding.   III, xxiii, 6

But we ought not to omit what he [Augustine] adds immediately thereafter: "For as we know not who belongs to the number of the predestined or who does not belong, we ought to be so minded as to wish that all men be saved." So shall it come about that we try to make everyone we meet a sharer in our peace. But our peace will rest upon the sons of peace. Hence, as far as we are concerned, . . . a healthful and severe rebuke should be applied as a medicine to all that they may not either perish themselves or destroy others. It belongs to God, however, to make that rebuke useful to those whom he . . . has foreknown and predestined.   III, xxiii, 14

PREDESTINATION, GOD'S WILL IN

As Scripture, then, clearly shows, we say that God once established by his eternal and unchangeable plan those whom he long before determined once for all to receive into salvation, and those whom, on the other hand, he would devote to destruction. We assert that, with respect to the elect, this plan was founded upon his freely given mercy, without regard to human worth; but by his just and irreprehensible but incomprehensible judgment he has barred the door of life to those whom he has given over to damnation. Now among the elect we regard the call as a testimony of election. Then we hold justification another sign of its manifestation, until they come into the glory in which the fulfillment of that election lies.   III, xxi, 7

Therefore he [Paul] answers without circumlocutions: God shows favor to his elect because he so wills; he has mercy upon them because he so wills. Accordingly, that declaration prevails: "I will show mercy on whom I will show mercy, and I will take pity on whom I will take pity," as if he said: "God is moved to mercy for no other reason but that he wills to be merciful." Then that saying of Augustine remains true: "God's grace does not find but makes those fit to be chosen."   III, xxii, 8

If, then, we cannot determine a reason why he vouchsafes mercy to his own, except that it so pleases him, neither shall we have any reason for rejecting others, other than his will. For when it is said that God hardens or shows mercy to whom he wills, men are warned by this to seek no cause outside his will.   III, xxii, 11

PREDESTINATION, WORD OF GOD AND

Let this, therefore, first of all be before our eyes: to seek any other knowledge of predestination than what the Word of God discloses is not less insane than if one should purpose to walk in a pathless waste, or to see in darkness.   III, xxi, 2

PREDESTINATION, WORKS AND

"The Father has predestined those whom he has chosen in himself to conform to the image of his Son that Christ may be the first-born among all the brethren." Therefore, "neither death, . . . nor things present, nor things to come, . . . will separate us from the love of God which is in Christ"; but rather all things will turn to our good and salvation. Take note that we do not justify man by works before God, but all who are of God we speak of as being "reborn," and as becoming "a new creation," so that they pass from the realm of sin into the realm of righteousness; and we say that by this testimony they confirm their calling, and, like trees, are judged by their fruits.   III, xv, 8

PRIDE

Strange and monstrous indeed is the license of our pride!

II, iii, 9

PROGRESS

But no one in this earthly prison of the body has sufficient strength to press on with due eagerness, and weakness so weighs down the greater number that, with wavering and limping and even creeping along the ground, they move at a feeble rate. Let each one of us, then, proceed according to the measure of his puny capacity and set out upon the journey we have begun. No one shall set out so inauspiciously as not daily to make some headway, though it be slight. Therefore, let us not cease so to act that we may make some unceasing progress in the way of the Lord. And let us not despair at the slightness of our success; for even though attainment may not correspond to desire, when today outstrips yesterday the effort is not lost. Only let us look toward our mark with sincere simplicity and aspire to our goal; not fondly flattering ourselves, nor excusing our own evil deeds, but with continuous effort striving toward this end: that we may surpass ourselves in goodness until we attain to goodness itself. It is this, indeed, which through the whole course of life we seek and follow. But we shall attain it only when we have cast off the weakness of the body, and are received into full fellowship with him.   III, vi, 5

PROVIDENCE

At the outset, then, let my readers grasp that providence means not that by which God idly observes from heaven what takes place on earth, but that by which, as keeper of the keys, he governs all events.   I, xvi, 4

From this we gather that his general providence not only flourishes among creatures so as to continue the order of nature, but is by his wonderful plan adapted to a definite and proper end.

I, xvi, 7

Yet since the sluggishness of our mind lies far beneath the height of God's providence, we must employ a distinction to lift it up. Therefore I shall put it this way: however all things may be ordained by God's purpose and sure distribution, for us they are fortuitous. Not that we think that fortune rules the world and men, tumbling all things at random up and down, for it is fitting that this folly be absent from the Christian's breast! But since the order, reason, end, and necessity of those things which happen for the most part lie hidden in God's purpose, and are not apprehended by human opinion, those things, which it is certain take place by God's will, are in a sense fortuitous. For they bear on the face of them no other appearance, whether they are considered in their own nature or weighed according to our knowledge and judgment. Let us imagine, for example, a merchant who, entering a wood with a company of faithful men, unwisely wanders away from his companions, and in his wandering comes upon a robber's den, falls among thieves, and is slain. His death was not only foreseen by God's eye, but also determined by his decree. For it is not said that he foresaw how long the life of each man would extend, but that he determined and fixed the bounds that men cannot pass. Yet as far as the capacity of our mind is concerned, all things therein seem fortuitous. What will a Christian think at this point? Just this: whatever happened in a death of this sort he will regard as fortuitous by nature, as it is; yet he will not doubt that God's providence exercised authority over fortune in directing its end. The same reckoning applies to the contingency of future events. As all future events are uncertain to us, so we hold them in suspense, as if they might incline to one side or the other. Yet in our hearts it nonetheless remains fixed that nothing will take place that the Lord has not previously foreseen.   I, XVI, 9

Therefore the Christian heart, since it has been thoroughly persuaded that all things happen by God's plan, and that nothing takes place by chance, will ever look to him as the principal cause of things, yet will give attention to the secondary causes in their proper place. . . . Gratitude of mind for the favorable outcome of things, patience in adversity, and also incredible freedom from worry about the future all necessarily follow upon this knowledge. Therefore whatever shall happen prosperously and according to the desire of his heart, God's servant will attribute wholly to God, whether he feels God's beneficence through the ministry of men, or has been helped by inanimate creatures. For thus he will reason in his mind; surely it is the Lord who has inclined their hearts to me, who has so bound them to me that they should become the instruments of his kindness toward me.   I, XVII, 6–7

Meanwhile, nevertheless, a godly man will not overlook the secondary causes. And indeed, he will not, just because he thinks those from whom he has received benefit are ministers of the divine goodness, pass them over, as if they had deserved no thanks for their human kindness; but from the bottom of his heart will feel himself beholden to them, willingly confess his obligation, and earnestly try as best he can to render thanks and as occasion presents itself.   I, XVII, 9

To sum up, since God's will is said to be the cause of all things, I have made his providence the determinative principle for all human plans and works, not only in order to display its force in the elect, who are ruled by the Holy Spirit, but also to compel the reprobate to obedience.   I, XVIII, 2

PURGATORY

One could for a time perhaps in a way conceal the fact that it was devised apart from God's Word in curious and bold rashness; that men believed in it by some sort of "revelations" forged by Satan's craft; and that some passages of Scripture were ignorantly distorted to confirm it. Still, the Lord does not allow man's effrontery so to break in upon the secret places of his judgments; and he sternly forbade that men, to the neglect of his Word, should inquire after truth from the dead. Neither does he allow his Word to be so irreligiously corrupted. . . . For what means this purgatory of theirs but that satisfaction for sins is paid by the souls of the dead after their death? Hence, when the notion of satisfaction is destroyed, purgatory itself is straightway torn up by the very roots. But if it is perfectly clear from our preceding discourse that the blood of Christ is the sole satisfaction for the sins of believers, the sole expiation, the sole purgation, what remains but to say that purgatory is simply a dreadful blasphemy against Christ? I pass over the sacrileges by which it is daily defended, the minor offenses that it breeds in religion, and innumerable other things that we see have come forth from such a fountain of impiety.   III, v, 6

When my adversaries, therefore, raise against me the objection that prayers for the dead have been a custom for thirteen hundred years, I ask them, in turn, by what word of God, by what revelation, by what example, is this done? . . . But that which derived from perverse emulation was so constantly increased by new additions that to help the dead in distress became the papacy's principal mark of holiness. But Scripture supplies another far better and more perfect solace when it testifies: "Blessed are the dead who die in the Lord." And it adds the reason: "Henceforth they rest from their labors." . . . Now, since the entire law and gospel do not furnish so much as a single syllable of leave to pray for the dead, it is to profane the invocation of God to attempt more than he has bidden us.   III, v, 10

PURITY

Indeed, if we should have to judge from our works how the Lord feels toward us, for my part, I grant that we can in no way attain it by conjecture. But since faith ought to correspond to a simple and free promise, no place for doubting is left. For with

what sort of confidence will we be armed, I pray, if we reason that
God is favorable to us provided our purity of life so merit it?

III, ii, 38

REASON

Since reason, therefore, by which man distinguishes between good
and evil, and by which he understands and judges, is a natural gift,
it could not be completely wiped out; but it was partly weakened
and partly corrupted, so that its misshapen ruins appear.

When we so condemn human understanding for its perpetual
blindness as to leave it no perception of any object whatever, we
not only go against God's Word, but also run counter to the experience of common sense.

Yet the fact remains that some seed of political order has been
implanted in all men. And this is ample proof that in the arrange-
ment of this life no man is without the light of reason.

II, ii, 12–13

To sum up: We see among all mankind that reason is proper to
our nature; it distinguishes us from brute beasts, just as they by
possessing feeling differ from inanimate things.   II, ii, 17

REASON, HOLY SPIRIT AND

Is our diligence, insight, understanding, and carefulness so completely corrupted that we can devise or prepare nothing right in
God's eyes? No wonder that it seems too hard for us who grudgingly
suffer ourselves to be deprived of keenness of reason, which we
count the most precious gift of all! But to the Holy Spirit who
"knows that all the thoughts of the wise are futile" and who clearly
declares that "every imagination of the human heart is solely evil"
it seems most fitting. If whatever our nature conceives, instigates,
undertakes, and attempts is always evil, how can that which is
pleasing to God, to whom holiness and righteousness alone are acceptable, even enter our minds?   II, ii, 25

REASON, SCRIPTURE AND

Human reason, therefore, neither approaches, nor strives toward, nor even takes a straight aim at, this truth: to understand who the true God is or what sort of God he wishes to be toward us. But we are drunk with the false opinion of our own insight and are thus extremely reluctant to admit that it is utterly blind and stupid in divine matters. Hence, it will be more effective, I believe, to prove this fact by Scriptural testimonies than by reasons.   II, ii, 18–19

RELIGION

Therefore it is utterly vain for some men to say that religion was invented by the subtlety and craft of a few to hold the simple folk in thrall by this device and that those very persons who originated the worship of God for others did not in the least believe that any God existed. I confess, indeed, that in order to hold men's minds in greater subjection, clever men have devised very many things in religion by which to inspire the common folk with reverence and to strike them with terror. But they would never have achieved this if men's minds had not already been imbued with a firm conviction about God, from which the inclination toward religion springs as from a seed.   I, iii, 2

REPENTANCE, CAUSES OF

It is for a very good reason that the apostle enumerates seven causes, effects, or parts in his description of repentance. They are earnestness or carefulness, excuse, indignation, fear, longing, zeal, and avenging. It should not seem absurd that I dare not determine whether they ought to be accounted causes or effects, for either is debatable.   III, iii, 15

REPENTANCE, CONFESSION AND

Now, while it is not always necessary to make men open and conscious witnesses of our repentance, yet to confess to God privately is a part of true repentance that cannot be omitted.   III, iii, 18

REPENTANCE, FAITH AND

Now it ought to be a fact beyond controversy that repentance not only constantly follows faith, but is also born of faith.   III, iii, 1

Yet, when we refer the origin of repentance to faith we do not imagine some space of time during which it brings it to birth; but we mean to show that a man cannot apply himself seriously to repentance without knowing himself to belong to God. But no one is truly persuaded that he belongs to God unless he has first recognized God's grace.   III, iii, 2

REPENTANCE, GOD'S ACTION IN

The gist of it is that God is without doubt ready to forgive, as soon as the sinner is converted. Therefore, in so far as God wills the sinner's repentance, he does not will his death.   III, xxiv, 15

REPENTANCE, REGENERATION AND

Therefore, in a word, I interpret repentance as regeneration, whose sole end is to restore in us the image of God that had been disfigured and all but obliterated through Adam's transgression.
III, iii, 9

REPENTANCE, SIGNS OF

We see "gospel repentance" in all those who, made sore by the sting of sin but aroused and refreshed by trust in God's mercy, have turned to the Lord.   III, iii, 4

REPROBATE

The fact that the reprobate do not obey God's Word when it is made known to them will be justly charged against the malice and depravity of their hearts, provided it be added at the same time that they have been given over to this depravity because they have been raised up by the just but inscrutable judgment of God to show forth his glory in their condemnation.   III, xxiv, 14

REST
We must be wholly at rest that God may work in us.

II, VIII, 29

RESURRECTION, BENEFITS OF
Next comes the resurrection from the dead. Without this what we have said so far would be incomplete. For since only weakness appears in the cross, death, and burial of Christ, faith must leap over all these things to attain its full strength. . . . Therefore, we divide the substance of our salvation between Christ's death and resurrection as follows: through his death, sin was wiped out and death extinguished; through his resurrection, righteousness was restored and life raised up, so that—thanks to his resurrection—his death manifested its power and efficacy in us. . . . We also receive a third benefit from his resurrection: we are assured of our own resurrection by receiving a sort of guarantee substantiated by his.

II, XVI, 13

Therefore, Christ rose again that he might have us as companions in the life to come.   III, xxv, 3

RESURRECTION, DEATH AND
Why the sacred and inviolable custom of burial but as an earnest of new life . . . ? If souls did not outlive bodies, what is it that has God present when it is separated from the body?   III, xxv, 5–6

RESURRECTION, GOD'S GLORY IN THE
But let us remember that no one is truly persuaded of the coming resurrection unless he is seized with wonder, and ascribes to the power of God its due glory. . . . Therefore, after Paul's example let us now eagerly triumph in the midst of our battles, because He who has promised us a future life is able to preserve what has been entrusted; and so let us exult that the crown of righteousness has been laid up for us, which the righteous Judge shall give to us.

III, xxv, 4

RESURRECTION, MEDITATION UPON

Accordingly, he alone has fully profited in the gospel who has accustomed himself to continual meditation upon the blessed resurrection.   III, xxv, 1

RESURRECTION OF THE BODY

Equally monstrous is the error of those who imagine that the souls will not receive the same bodies with which they are now clothed but will be furnished with new and different ones. . . . For it would be utterly absurd that the bodies which God has dedicated to himself as temples should fall away into filth without hope of resurrection!   III, xxv, 7

First, we must hold, as I have indicated, that as to substance we shall be raised again in the same flesh we now bear, but that the quality will be different. So it was that, when the same flesh of Christ which had been offered as a sacrifice was raised up, it yet excelled in other gifts as if it had become utterly different. . . . Since God has all the elements ready at his bidding, no difficulty will hinder his commanding earth, waters, and fire to restore what they seem to have consumed.   III, xxv, 8

REVENGE

For if it is a civil case, a man does not take the right path unless he commits his cause, with innocent simplicity, to the judge as public protector; and he should think not at all of returning evil for evil, which is the passion for revenge. If, however, the action is brought for some capital or serious offense, we require that the accuser be one who comes into court without a burning desire for revenge or resentment over private injury, but having in mind only to prevent the efforts of a destructive man from doing harm to society. For if you remove a vengeful mind, that command which forbids revenge to Christians is not broken.   IV, xx, 19

RICHES

They who have narrow and slender resources should know how to go without things patiently, lest they be troubled by an immoderate desire for them.   III, x, 5

RIGHTEOUSNESS, ADOPTION AND

For we have been adopted as sons by the Lord with this one condition: that our life express Christ, the bond of our adoption. Accordingly, unless we give and devote ourselves to righteousness, we not only revolt from our Creator with wicked perfidy but we also abjure our Savior himself.   III, vi, 3

RIGHTEOUSNESS, IMPERFECT

In all ages this irreligious affectation of religion, because it is rooted in man's nature, has manifested itself and still manifests itself; for men always delight in contriving some way of acquiring righteousness apart from God's Word.   II, viii, 5

RIGHTEOUSNESS, KINDS OF

To make this matter clearer, let us examine what kind of righteousness is possible to man through the whole course of his life; let us, indeed, make a fourfold classification of it. For men are either (1) endowed with no knowledge of God and immersed in idolatry, or (2) initiated into the sacraments, yet by impurity of life denying God in their actions while they confess him with their lips, they belong to Christ only in name; or (3) they are hypocrites who conceal with empty pretenses their wickedness of heart, or (4) regenerated by God's Spirit, they make true holiness their concern.

III, xiv, 1

RIGHTEOUSNESS, LAW AND

The law has been divinely handed down to us to teach us perfect righteousness.   II, viii, 5

RIGHTEOUSNESS, PERFECT

We therefore willingly confess that perfect obedience to the law is righteousness, and that the keeping of each commandment is a part of righteousness; provided that in the remaining parts the whole sum of righteousness is contained. But we deny that such a form of righteousness exists anywhere.   III, xvii, 7

RITUAL
It is certain that all ceremonies are corrupt and harmful unless through them men are led to Christ.   IV, x, 15

SACRAMENT, A MIRROR (see MIRROR)

SACRAMENT, A SYMBOL
Indeed, the believer, when he sees the sacraments with his own eyes, does not halt at the physical sight of them, but by those steps (which I have indicated by analogy) rises up in devout contemplation to those lofty mysteries which lie hidden in the sacraments.

IV, xiv, 5

SACRAMENT, DEFINITION OF
First, we must consider what a sacrament is. It seems to me that a simple and proper definition would be to say that it is an outward sign by which the Lord seals on our consciences the promises of his good will toward us in order to sustain the weakness of our faith; and we in turn attest our piety toward him in the presence of the Lord and of his angels and before men. Here is another briefer definition: one may call it a testimony of divine grace toward us, confirmed by an outward sign, with mutual attestation of our piety toward him.   IV, xiv, 1

SACRAMENTS, GRACE AND
I say only this: God uses means and instruments which he himself sees to be expedient, that all things may serve his glory, since he is Lord and Judge of all. He feeds our bodies through bread and other foods, he illumines the world through the sun, and he warms it through heat; yet neither bread, nor sun, nor fire, is anything save in so far as he distributes his blessings to us by these instruments. In like manner, he nourishes faith spiritually through the sacraments, whose one function is to set his promises before our eyes to be looked upon, indeed, to be guarantees of them to us. It

is our duty to put no confidence in other creatures which have been destined for our use by God's generosity and beneficence, and through whose ministry he lavishes the gifts of his bounty upon us; nor to admire and proclaim them as the causes of our good. In the same way, neither ought our confidence to inhere in the sacraments, nor the glory of God be transferred to them. Rather, laying aside all things, both our faith and our confession ought to rise up to him who is the author of the sacraments and of all things.   IV, xiv, 12

Water is sometimes drunk from a spring, sometimes drawn, sometimes led by channels to water the fields, yet it does not flow forth from itself for so many uses, but from the very source, which by unceasing flow supplies and serves it. In like manner, the flesh of Christ is like a rich and inexhaustible fountain that pours into us the life springing forth from the Godhead into itself. Now who does not see that communion of Christ's flesh and blood is necessary for all who aspire to heavenly life?   IV, xvii, 9

SACRAMENTS, HOLY SPIRIT AND

As to the confirmation and increase of faith (which I think I have already explained in clear terms), I should therefore like my readers to be reminded that I assign this particular ministry to the sacraments. Not that I suppose there is some secret force or other perpetually seated in them by which they are able to promote or confirm faith by themselves. Rather, I consider that they have been instituted by the Lord to the end that they may serve to establish and increase faith. But the sacraments properly fulfill their office only when the Spirit, that inward teacher, comes to them, by whose power alone hearts are penetrated and affections moved and our souls opened for the sacraments to enter in.   IV, xiv, 9

SACRAMENTS, MERITS OF

It is good that our readers be briefly apprized of this thing also; whatever the Sophists have dreamed up concerning the *opus operatum* is not only false but contradicts the nature of the sacraments, which God so instituted that believers, poor and deprived of all goods, should bring nothing to it but begging. From this it follows that in receiving the sacraments believers do nothing to deserve praise, and that even in this act (which on their part is merely passive) no work can be ascribed to them. IV, xiv, 26

SACRAMENTS, PROMISE IN

First, it is a doctrine well enough known and confessed among all godly men that a right consideration of signs does not rest solely in external ceremonies, but depends chiefly upon the promise and the spiritual mysteries, which the Lord ordains the ceremonies themselves to represent. IV, xvi, 2

SACRAMENTS, SALVATION AND

Assurance of salvation does not depend upon participation in the sacrament, as if justification consisted in it. For we know that justification is lodged in Christ alone, and that it is communicated to us no less by the preaching of the gospel than by the seal of the sacrament, and without the latter can stand unimpaired.

IV, xiv, 14

SACRAMENT, WORD OF GOD AND

It is therefore certain that the Lord offers us mercy and the pledge of his grace both in his Sacred Word and in his sacraments. But it is understood only by those who take Word and sacraments with sure faith, just as Christ is offered and held forth by the Father to all unto salvation, yet not all acknowledge and receive him.

IV, xiv, 7

Therefore, let it be regarded as a settled principle that the sacraments have the same office as the Word of God: to offer and set forth Christ to us, and in him the treasures of heavenly grace. But they avail and profit nothing unless received in faith. IV, xiv, 17

The Word of God must precede, to make a sacrament a sacrament, as Augustine very well states. IV, xix, 2

SACRIFICE, CHRIST'S

In short, the only reason given in Scripture that the Son of God willed to take our flesh, and accepted this commandment from the Father, is that he would be a sacrifice to appease the Father on our behalf.   II, xii, 4

And truly, even in death itself his willing obedience is the important thing because a sacrifice not offered voluntarily would not have furthered righteousness.   II, xvi, 5

I say that nothing is more apparent than that Christ's sacrifice is alone sufficient to forgive the voluntary sins of the saints inasmuch as the Lord has attested this by carnal sacrifices as seals.   IV, i, 28

Therefore, we shall have to confess either that Christ's sacrifice, which he fulfilled upon the cross, lacked the power to cleanse eternally, or that Christ had carried out one sacrifice, once for all, unto all ages.   IV, xviii, 3

SAINTS, COMMUNION OF

Accordingly, "the communion of saints" is added. This clause, though generally omitted by the ancients, ought not to be overlooked, for it very well expresses what the church is. It is as if one said that the saints are gathered into the society of Christ on the principle that whatever benefits God confers upon them, they should in turn share with one another.   IV, i, 3

SAINTS, FAULTS OF

For the church fathers well knew that the saints often totter in unbelief, sometimes give vent to superfluous oaths, now and then flare into anger, indeed, even break out into open railing, and besides are troubled with other ills that the Lord thoroughly abominates.

IV, i, 29

SALVATION

Salvation has been prepared only for those whom the Lord deems worthy of his mercy, while ruin and death remain for all those whom He has not chosen.   II, v, 17

For so he [Paul] speaks to the Romans: "All have sinned and lack the glory of God; moreover, they are justified freely by his grace." Here you have the head and primal source: that God embraced us with his free mercy.   III, xiv, 17

For we have it from the words of the apostle that the salvation of believers has been founded upon the decision of divine election alone, and that this favor is not earned by works but comes from free calling.   III, xxii, 5

Now, it is very important for us to know what benefit we shall gain from this. The basis on which we believe the church is that we are fully convinced we are members of it. In this way our salvation rests upon sure and firm supports, so that, even if the whole fabric of the world were overthrown, the church could neither totter nor fall. First, it stands by God's election, and cannot waver or fail any more than his eternal providence can. Secondly, it has in a way been joined to the steadfastness of Christ, who will no more allow his believers to be estranged from him than that his members be rent and torn asunder.   IV, i, 3

SANCTIFICATION

As soon as any very wicked person has performed one or another of the duties of the law, he does not doubt that it will be accounted to him as righteousness; but the Lord proclaims that no sanctification can be acquired from this action unless the heart has first been well cleansed. And not content with this, he declares that all the works that come forth from sinners are contaminated with impurity of heart. Take, then, the name of righteousness from those works which are condemned as works of pollution by the Lord's mouth!
III, xiv, 7

SARCASM

For whence came the beginning of idols but from the opinion of men? Most just is that profane poet's mockery: "Once I was a little

fig tree trunk, a useless bit of wood, when the workman, in doubt
whether he should make a stool, preferred that I be a god," etc.
I, xi, 4

SATAN (see also DEVIL, LIMITATION OF)

Therefore, whatever men or Satan himself may instigate, God
nevertheless holds the key, so that he turns their efforts to carry out
his judgments. . . . I confess, indeed, that it is often by means
of Satan's intervention that God acts in the wicked, but in such a
way that Satan performs his part by God's impulsion and advances
as far as he is allowed.   I, xviii, 1–2

But because that promise to crush Satan's head pertains to Christ
and all his members in common, I deny that believers can ever be
conquered or overwhelmed by him. Often, indeed, are they dis-
tressed, but not so deprived of life as not to recover; they fall under
violent blows, but afterward they are raised up; they are wounded,
but not fatally, in short, they so toil throughout life that at the
last they obtain the victory. . . . In our Head, indeed, this victory
always fully existed, for the prince of the world had nothing in him.
Moreover, it now appears in part in us, who are his members; it will
be completed when we shall have put off our flesh, in respect to
which we are as yet subject to infirmity, and will be filled with the
power of the Holy Spirit.   I, xiv, 18

SCRIPTURE, AUTHORITY OF

For by his Word, God rendered faith unambiguous forever, a faith
that should be superior to all opinion.   I, vi, 2

The whole power of earth has armed itself to destroy it [the
Scripture], yet all these efforts have gone up in smoke. How could it,
assailed so strongly from every side, have resisted if it had relied
upon human protection alone? Rather, by this very fact, it is
proved to be from God, because, with all human efforts striving
against it, still it has of its own power thus far prevailed. Besides
this, it is not one state, not one people, that has agreed to receive
and embrace it; but, as far and as wide as the earth extends, it has

obtained its authority by the holy concord of divers peoples, who otherwise had nothing in common among themselves. Such agreement of minds, so disparate and otherwise disagreeing in everything among themselves, ought to move us greatly, since it is clear that this agreement is brought about by nothing else than the divine will. Yet no little weight is added thereto when we observe the godliness of those who so agree, not of all, indeed, but of those whom the Lord has made to shine as lamps in his church.

I, viii, 12

SCRIPTURE, BENEFIT OF

Indeed, the Word of God is like the sun, shining upon all those to whom it is proclaimed, but with no effect among the blind.

III, ii, 34

SCRIPTURE, FAITH AND

The same Word is the basis whereby faith is supported and sustained; if it turns away from the Word, it falls. Therefore, take away the Word and no faith will then remain.   III, ii, 6

SCRIPTURE, GUIDANCE OF

For just as eyes, when dimmed with age or weakness or by some other defect, unless aided by spectacles, discern nothing distinctly; so, such is our feebleness, unless Scripture guides us in seeking God, we are immediately confused.   I, xiv, 1

SCRIPTURE, HOLY SPIRIT AND

Let this point therefore stand: that those whom the Holy Spirit has inwardly taught truly rest upon Scripture, and that Scripture indeed is self-authenticated, hence, it is not right to subject it to proof and reasoning.   I, vii, 5

Therefore Scripture will ultimately suffice for a saving knowledge of God only when its certainty is founded upon the inward persuasion of the Holy Spirit. Indeed, these human testimonies which exist

to confirm it will not be vain if, as secondary aids to our feebleness, they follow that chief and highest testimony. But those who
wish to prove to unbelievers that Scripture is the Word of God are
acting foolishly, for only by faith can this be known.   I, VIII, 13

For Scripture is the school of the Holy Spirit, in which, as nothing
is omitted that is both necessary and useful to know, so nothing is
taught but what is expedient to know.   III, XXI, 3

SCRIPTURE, HOW TO READ
Yes, if we turn pure eyes and upright senses toward it, the majesty
of God will immediately come to view, subdue our bold rejection,
and compel us to obey.   I, VII, 4

SCRIPTURE, INTERPRETATION OF
But as for us, we study with no less obedience than care to obtain
a sound understanding of this passage, as we do in the whole of
Scripture. And we do not with perverted ardor and without discrimination rashly seize upon what first springs to our minds.
Rather, after diligently meditating upon it, we embrace the meaning
which the Spirit of God offers. Relying upon it, we look down
from a height at whatever of earthly wisdom is set against it. Indeed, we hold our minds captive, that they dare not raise even one
little word of protest; and humble them, that they dare not rebel
against it. From this has arisen our explanation of Christ's words
which even all those moderately versed in Scripture know from un-
varying Biblical usage to be common to the sacraments.
                                                            IV, XVII, 25

SCRIPTURE, PROOF OF
Thus, the highest proof of Scripture derives in general from the
fact that God in person speaks in it.   I, VII, 4

SCRIPTURE, PURPOSE OF
Just as old or bleary-eyed men and those with weak vision, if you
thrust before them a most beautiful volume, even if they recognize

it to be some sort of writing, yet can scarcely construe two words, but with the aid of spectacles will begin to read distinctly; so Scripture, gathering up the otherwise confused knowledge of God in our minds, having dispersed our dullness, clearly shows us the true God.   I, vi, 1

SCRIPTURE, QUICKENING POWER OF

I take it for granted that there is such life energy in God's Word that it quickens the souls of all to whom God grants participation in it.   II, x, 7

SCRIPTURE, REVELATION OF GOD IN

That brightness which is borne in upon the eyes of all men both in heaven and on earth is more than enough to withdraw all support from men's ingratitude—just as God, to involve the human race in the same guilt, sets forth to all without exception his presence portrayed in his creatures. Despite this, it is needful that another and better help be added to direct us aright to the very Creator of the universe. It was not in vain, then, that he added the light of his Word by which to become known unto salvation.   I, vi, 1

SCRIPTURE, TRUTH OF

Indeed, Scripture exhibits fully as clear evidence of its own truth as white and black things do of their color, or sweet and bitter things do of their taste.   I, vii, 2

Now since such uncultivated and almost rude simplicity inspires greater reverence for itself than any eloquence, what ought one to conclude except that the force of the truth of Sacred Scripture is manifestly too powerful to need the art of words?   I, viii, 1

SCRIPTURE, UNITY OF

What then? You will ask: will no difference remain between the Old and New Testaments? What is to become of the many passages of Scripture wherein they are contrasted as utterly different? I freely admit the differences in Scripture, to which attention is called, but in such a way as not to detract from its established unity. This will become apparent when we have discussed them in their order.

II, xi, 1

SCRIPTURE, WORD OF GOD

Let this be a firm principle: No other word is to be held as the Word of God, and given place as such in the church, than what is contained first in the Law and the Prophets, then in the writings of the apostles; and the only authorized way of teaching in the church is by the prescription and standard of his Word.   IV, viii, 8

This, then, is the difference. Our opponents locate the authority of the church outside God's Word; but we insist that it be attached to the Word, and do not allow it to be separated from it.   IV, viii, 13

SCRIPTURE, WRITTEN FORM OF

Suppose we ponder how slippery is the fall of the human mind into forgetfulness of God, how great the tendency to every kind of error, how great the lust to fashion constantly new and artificial religions. Then we may perceive how necessary was such written proof of the heavenly doctrine, that it should neither perish through forgetfulness nor vanish through error nor be corrupted by the audacity of men.   I, vi, 3

SELFISHNESS

Hence it is very clear that we keep the commandments not by loving ourselves but by loving God and neighbor; that he lives the best and holiest life who lives and strives for himself as little as he can, and that no one lives in a worse or more evil manner than he who lives and strives for himself alone, and thinks about and seeks only his own advantage.   II, viii, 54

There is no other remedy than to tear out from our inward parts this most deadly pestilence of love of strife and love of self, even as it is plucked out by Scriptural teaching. For thus we are instructed to remember that those talents which God has bestowed upon us are not our own goods but the free gifts of God; and any persons who become proud of them show their ungratefulness.   III, vii, 4

SENSES

Therefore I admit in the first place that there are five senses, which Plato preferred to call organs, by which all objects are presented to common sense, as a sort of receptacle. There follows fantasy, which distinguishes those things which have been apprehended by common sense; then reason, which embraces universal judgment; finally understanding, which in intent and quiet study contemplates what reason discursively ponders.   I, xv, 6

SERVETUS

But in our own age too, a no less deadly monster has emerged, Michael Servetus, who has supposed the Son of God to be a figment compounded from God's essence, spirit, flesh, and three uncreated elements. First of all, he denies that Christ is the Son of God for any other reason than that he was begotten of the Holy Spirit in the virgin's womb. His subtlety takes this direction: having overturned the distinction of the two natures, he regards Christ to be a mixture of some divine and some human elements, but not to be reckoned both God and man.   II, xiv, 5

For Servetus the name "Trinity" was so utterly hateful and detestable that he commonly labeled all those whom he called Trinitarians as atheists.   I, xiii, 22

The impiety of Servetus was even more detestable, when he asserted that God was never revealed to Abraham and the other patriarchs, but that in his place an angel was worshiped.
     I, xiii, 10

Yet we ought to beware of the devilish imagination of Servetus, who—while he wishes to extol the greatness of Christ's grace or at least pretends to wish this—entirely abolishes the promises, as if they had ended at the same time as the law.   II, IX, 3

His fourth objection is that because what is physical comes first, we must await a mature time for baptism, which is spiritual. But though I admit that all the offspring of Adam begotten of flesh bear their condemnation from the very womb itself, I still deny that this prevents God from providing an immediate remedy. For Servetus will not prove that many years were divinely prescribed for the newness of spiritual life to begin. As Paul testifies, although those who are born of believers may by nature be lost, they are holy by supernatural grace.   IV, XVI, 31

SERVICE
I call "service" not only what lies in obedience to God's Word but what turns the mind of man, empty of its own carnal sense, wholly to the bidding of God's Spirit.   III, VII, 1

SIN, DEFINITION OF
We, on the other hand, deem it sin when man is tickled by any desire at all against the law of God.   III, III, 10

SIN, HOLY SPIRIT AND
But even while by the leading of the Holy Spirit we walk in the ways of the Lord, to keep us from forgetting ourselves and becoming puffed up, traces of our imperfection remain to give us occasion for humility.   III, XIV, 9

SIN, MAN SUBJECT TO
Therefore let us hold this as an undoubted truth which no siege engines can shake: the mind of man has been so completely es-

tranged from God's righteousness that it conceives, desires, and undertakes, only that which is impious, perverted, foul, impure, and infamous. The heart is so steeped in the poison of sin, that it can breathe out nothing but a loathsome stench. But if some men occasionally make a show of good, their minds nevertheless ever remain enveloped in hypocrisy and deceitful craft, and their hearts bound by inner perversity.   II, v, 19.

SIN, ORIGINAL

This is the inherited corruption, which the church fathers termed "original sin," meaning by the word "sin" the depravation of a nature previously good and pure. . . . Therefore all of us, who have descended from impure seed, are born infected with the contagion of sin. In fact, before we saw the light of this life we were soiled and spotted in God's sight.   II, i, 5

These are no obscure words: "Many are made righteous by Christ's obedience as by Adam's disobedience they had been made sinners." Here, then, is the relationship between the two: Adam, implicating us in his ruin, destroyed us with himself; but Christ restores us to salvation by his grace.   II, i, 6

So that these remarks may not be made concerning an uncertain and unknown matter, let us define original sin. It is not my intention to investigate the several definitions proposed by various writers, but simply to bring forward the one that appears to me most in accordance with truth. Original sin, therefore, seems to be a hereditary depravity and corruption of our nature, diffused into all parts of the soul, which first makes us liable to God's wrath, then also brings forth in us those works which Scripture calls "works of the flesh." And that is properly what Paul often calls sin.   II, i, 8

Now, it is clear how false is the teaching, long propagated by some and still persisted in by others, that through baptism we are released and made exempt from original sin, and from the corruption that descended from Adam into all his posterity; and are restored into that same righteousness and purity of nature which

Adam would have obtained if he had remained upright as he was first created. For teachers of this type never understood what original sin, what original righteousness, or what the grace of baptism was.

IV, xv, 10

SIN, PARDON OF

Therefore, in the communion of saints, our sins are continually forgiven us by the ministry of the church itself when the presbyters or bishops to whom this office has been committed strengthen godly consciences by the gospel promises in the hope of pardon and forgiveness. This they do both publicly and privately as need requires.

IV, i, 22

SIN, REIGN OF

So long as you live, sin must needs be in your members. At least let it be deprived of mastery. Let not what it bids be done.

III, iii, 13

SIN, RELICS OF

Accordingly, we say that the old man was so crucified, and the law of sin so abolished in the children of God, that some vestiges remain; not to rule over them, but to humble them by the consciousness of their own weakness.   III, iii, 11

SINGING

It is evident that the practice of singing in church, to speak also of this in passing, is not only a very ancient one but also was in use among the apostles. This we may infer from Paul's words: "I will sing with the spirit and I will sing with the mind." Likewise, Paul speaks to the Colossians: "Teaching and admonishing one another . . . in hymns, psalms, and spiritual songs, singing with thankfulness in your hearts to the Lord." . . . Yet we should be very careful that our ears be not more attentive to the melody than our minds to the spiritual meaning of the words.   III, xx, 32

SOUL

But the nimbleness of the human mind in searching out heaven and earth and the secrets of nature, and when all ages have been compassed by its understanding and memory, in arranging each thing in its proper order, and in inferring future events from past, clearly shows that there lies hidden in man something separate from the body. . . . Now, unless the soul were something essential, separate from the body, Scripture would not teach that we dwell in houses of clay and at death leave the tabernacle of the flesh, putting off what is corruptible so that at the Last Day we may finally receive our reward, according as each of us has done in the body.   I, xv, 2

SPECULATION

Finally, I trust that the whole sum of this doctrine has been faithfully explained, if my readers will impose a limit upon their curiosity, and not seek out for themselves more eagerly than is proper troublesome and perplexed disputations. For I suspect that those who intemperately delight in speculation will not be at all satisfied.
I, xiii, 29

STEALING

We will duly obey this [eighth] commandment, then, if, content with our lot, we are zealous to make only honest and lawful gain: if we do not seek to become wealthy through injustice, nor attempt to deprive our neighbor of his goods to increase our own; if we do not strive to heap up riches cruelly wrung from the blood of others; if we do not madly scrape together from everywhere, by fair means or foul, whatever will feed our avarice or satisfy our prodigality.
II, viii, 46

STEWARDSHIP

Let this, therefore, be our rule for generosity and beneficence: We are the stewards of everything God has conferred on us by which we are able to help our neighbor, and are required to render account of our stewardship. Moreover, the only right stewardship is that which is tested by the rule of love. Thus it will come about that we shall not only join zeal for another's benefit with care for our own advantage, but shall subordinate the latter to the former.

III, VII, 5

SUCCESS

Lastly, if things do not go according to our wish and hope, we will still be restrained from impatience and loathing of our condition, whatever it may be. For we shall know that this is to murmur against God, by whose will riches and poverty, contempt and honor, are dispensed. To sum up, he who rests solely upon the blessing of God, as it has been here expressed, will neither strive with evil arts after those things which men customarily madly seek after, which he realizes will not profit him, nor will he, if things go well, give credit to himself or even to his diligence, or industry, or fortune. Rather, he will give God the credit as its Author.   III, VII, 9

SUFFERING

For in times of adversity believers comfort themselves with the solace that they suffer nothing except by God's ordinance and command, for they are under his hand.   I, XVI, 3

For the Lord often leaves his servants not only to be troubled by the lust of the wicked but to be torn and destroyed. He lets good men languish in darkness and filth, while the wicked almost shine among the stars. And he does not so cheer them with the brightness of his countenance that they enjoy lasting happiness.   II, X, 16

We ought accordingly to be content with the testimony of Christ rather than with the false estimation of the flesh. So it will come about that we shall rejoice after the apostle's example, "whenever he will count us worthy to suffer dishonor for his name." What then? If, being innocent and of good conscience, we are stripped of our possessions by the wickedness of impious folk, we are indeed reduced to penury among men. But in God's presence in heaven our true riches are thus increased. If we are cast out of our own house, then we will be the more intimately received into God's family. If we are vexed and despised, we but take all the firmer root in Christ. If we are branded with disgrace and ignominy, we but have a fuller place in the Kingdom of God. If we are slain, entrance into the blessed life will thus be open to us. Let us be ashamed to esteem less than the shadowy and fleeting allurements of the present life, those things on which the Lord has set so great a value.   III, VIII, 7

SUNDAY

But we ought especially to hold to this general doctrine: that, in order to prevent religion from either perishing or declining among us, we should diligently frequent the sacred meetings, and make use of those external aids which can promote the worship of God.

II, VIII, 34

TEMPERANCE

Long ago Cato truly said: "There is great care about dress, but great carelessness about virtue." To use the old proverb: those who are much occupied with the care of the body are for the most part careless about their own souls.   III, x, 4

TEMPTATION

It makes very little difference whether we understand by the word "evil" the devil or sin. Indeed, Satan himself is the enemy who lies in wait for our life; moreover, he is armed with sin to destroy us. This, then, is our plea: that we may not be vanquished or overwhelmed by any temptations but may stand fast by the Lord's power against all hostile powers that attack us. This is not to succumb to temptations that, received into his care and safekeeping and secure in his protection, we may victoriously endure sin, death, the gates of hell, and the devil's whole kingdom. This is to be freed from evil.

III, xx, 46

TEN COMMANDMENTS

God has so divided his law into two parts, which contain the whole of righteousness, as to assign the first part to those duties of religion which particularly concern the worship of his majesty; the second, to the duties of love that have to do with men.   II, VIII, 11

TEN COMMANDMENTS (continued)

First

Therefore, in forbidding us to have strange gods, he means that we are not to transfer to another what belongs to him.   II, viii, 16

Second

In the previous commandment, he declared himself the one God, apart from whom no other gods are to be imagined or had. Now he declares more openly what sort of God he is, and with what kind of worship he should be honored, lest we dare attribute anything carnal to him.   II, viii, 17

Third

The purpose of this commandment is: God wills that we hallow the majesty of his name. Therefore, it means in brief that we are not to profane his name by treating it contemptuously and irreverently.
                                                                II, viii, 22

Fourth

The purpose of this commandment is that, being dead to our own inclinations and works, we should meditate on the Kingdom of God, and that we should practice that meditation in the ways established by him. But, since this commandment has a particular consideration distinct from the others, it requires a slightly different order of exposition. The early fathers customarily called this commandment a foreshadowing because it contains the outward keeping of a day which, upon Christ's coming, was abolished with the other figures. This they say truly, but they touch upon only half the matter. Hence, we must go deeper in our exposition, and ponder three conditions in which, it seems to me, the keeping of this commandment consists. First, under the repose of the seventh day the heavenly Lawgiver meant to represent to the people of Israel spiritual rest, in which believers ought to lay aside their own works to allow God to work in them. Secondly, he meant that there was to be a stated day for them to assemble to hear the law and perform the rites, or at least to devote it particularly to meditation upon his works, and thus through this remembrance to be trained in piety. Thirdly, he resolved to give a day of rest to servants and those who are under the authority of others, in order that they should have some respite from toil.   II, viii, 28

Fifth

The purpose is: since the maintenance of his economy pleases the Lord God, the degrees of pre-eminence established by him ought to be inviolable for us. This, then, is the sum: that we should look up to those whom God has placed over us, and should treat them with honor, obedience, and gratefulness.   II, VIII, 35

Sixth

The purpose of this commandment is: the Lord has bound mankind together by a certain unity; hence each man ought to concern himself with the safety of all. To sum up, then, all violence, injury, and any harmful thing at all that may injure our neighbor's body are forbidden to us.   II, VIII, 39

Seventh

The purpose of this commandment is: because God loves modesty and purity, all uncleanness must be far from us. To sum up, then: we should not become defiled with any filth or lustful intemperance of the flesh.   II, VIII, 41

Eighth

The purpose of this commandment is: since injustice is an abomination to God, we should render to each man what belongs to him. To sum up: we are forbidden to pant after the possessions of others, and consequently are commanded to strive faithfully to help every man to keep his own possessions.   II, VIII, 45

Ninth

The purpose of this commandment is: since God (who is truth) abhors a lie, we must practice truth without deceit toward one another. To sum up, then: let us not malign anyone with slanders or false charges, nor harm his substance by falsehood, in short, injure him by unbridled evilspeaking and impudence.   II, VIII, 47

Tenth

The purpose of this commandment is: since God wills that our whole soul be possessed with a disposition to love, we must banish from our hearts all desire contrary to love. To sum up, then: no thought should steal upon us to move our hearts to a harmful covetousness that tends to our neighbor's loss.   II, viii, 49

TESTAMENTS, DIFFERENCES IN THE

Now this is the first difference: the Lord of old willed that his people direct and elevate their minds to the heavenly heritage; yet, to nourish them better in this hope, he displayed it for them to see and, so to speak, taste, under earthly benefits. But now that the gospel has more plainly and clearly revealed the grace of the future life, the Lord leads our minds to meditate upon it directly, laying aside the lower mode of training that he used with the Israelites.
II, xi, 1

The second difference between the Old and New Testaments consists in figures: that, in the absence of the reality, it showed but an image and shadow in place of the substance; the New Testament reveals the very substance of truth as present.   II, xi, 4

"I will put my law within them, and I will write it upon their hearts . . . and I will forgive their iniquity. And each will not teach his neighbor, each man his brother. For all will know me, from the least to the greatest." From these words the apostle took occasion to make a comparison between the law and the gospel, calling the former literal, the latter spiritual doctrine; the former he speaks of as carved on tablets of stone, the latter as written upon men's hearts; the former is the preaching of death, the latter of life; the former of condemnation, the latter of righteousness; the former to be made void, the latter to abide.   II, xi, 7

The fourth difference arises out of the third. Scripture calls the Old Testament one of "bondage" because it produces fear in men's minds: but the New Testament, one of "freedom" because it lifts them to trust and assurance.   II, xi, 9

The fifth difference, which may be added, lies in the fact that until the advent of Christ, the Lord set apart one nation within which to confine the covenant of his grace.   II, xi, 11

THEOLOGIAN, DUTY OF THE
The theologian's task is not to divert the ears with chatter, but to strengthen consciences by teaching things true, sure, and profitable.

I, xiv, 4

TRANSUBSTANTIATION
They therefore had to take refuge in the fiction that a conversion of the bread into the body takes place; not that the body is properly made from the bread, but because Christ, to hide himself under the figure, annihilates its substance.   IV, xvii, 14

From this it is easily inferred that in earthly elements, when they are applied to a spiritual use, no other conversion occurs than with respect to men, inasmuch as to them they are seals of the promises.   IV, xvii, 15

TRINITY
And that they [the good doctors] might fortify themselves against his [Sabellius] tortuous cunning with the open and simple truth, they truly affirmed that a trinity of persons subsists in the one God, or, what was the same thing, subsists in the unity of God. . . . If, therefore, these terms were not rashly invented, we ought to beware lest by repudiating them we be accused of overweening rashness. Indeed, I could wish they were buried, if only among all men this faith were agreed on: that Father and Son and Spirit are one God, yet the Son is not the Father, nor the Spirit the Son, but that they are differentiated by a peculiar quality. Really, I am not, indeed, such a stickler as to battle doggedly over mere words. For I note that the ancients, who otherwise speak very reverently concerning these matters, agree neither among themselves nor even at all times individually with themselves. . . . Indeed, if anxious superstition so constrains anyone that he cannot bear these terms, yet no one could now deny, even if he were to burst, that when we hear "one" we ought to understand "unity of substance"; when we hear "three in one essence," the persons in this trinity are meant.   I, xiii, 4–5

And he [God] is not divided according to the distribution of gifts, but however diversely they may be divided; yet, says the apostle, he remains "one and the same". . . . And that passage in Gregory of Nazianzus vastly delights me: "I cannot think on the one without quickly being encircled by the splendor of the three; nor can I discern the three without being straightway carried back to the one."   I, xiii, 16–17

TRUST

For nothing so moves us to repose our assurance and certainty of mind in the Lord as distrust of ourselves, and the anxiety occasioned by the awareness of our ruin.   III, ii, 23

But in these matters the believer must also look to God's kindness and truly fatherly indulgence. Accordingly, if he sees his house reduced to solitude by the removal of his kinsfolk, he will not indeed even then cease to bless the Lord, but rather will turn his attention to this thought: nevertheless, the grace of the Lord, which dwells in my house, will not leave it desolate. Or, if his crops are blasted by frost, or destroyed by ice, or beaten down with hail, and he sees famine threatening, yet he will not despair or bear a grudge against God, but will remain firm in this trust: "Nevertheless we are in the Lord's protection, sheep brought up in his pastures." The Lord will therefore supply food to us even in extreme barrenness. If he shall be afflicted by disease, he will not even then be so unmanned by the harshness of pain as to break forth into impatience and expostulate with God; but, by considering the righteousness and gentleness of God's chastening, he will recall himself to forbearance. In short, whatever happens, because he will know it ordained of God, he will undergo it with a peaceful and grateful mind so as not obstinately to resist the command of him into whose power he once for all surrendered himself and his every possession. Especially let that foolish and most miserable consolation of the pagans be far away from the breast of the Christian man; to strengthen their minds against adversities, they charged these to fortune. Against fortune they considered it foolish to be angry because she was blind and unthinking, with unseeing eyes wounding the deserving and the undeserving at the same time. On the contrary, the rule of piety is

that God's hand alone is the judge and governor of fortune, good
or bad, and that it does not rush about with heedless force, but
with most orderly justice deals out good as well as ill to us.

III, vii, 10

TRUTH

Whenever we come upon these matters in secular writers, let that
admirable light of truth shining in them teach us that the mind
of man, though fallen and perverted from its wholeness, is nevertheless clothed and ornamented with God's excellent gifts. If we
regard the Spirit of God as the sole fountain of truth, we shall
neither reject the truth itself, nor despise it wherever it shall appear,
unless we wish to dishonor the Spirit of God. . . . But shall we
count anything praiseworthy or noble without recognizing at the
same time that it comes from God . . . ? Those men whom Scripture calls "natural men" were, indeed, sharp and penetrating in
their investigation of inferior things. Let us, accordingly, learn by
their example how many gifts the Lord left to human nature even
after it was despoiled of its true good.   II, ii, 15

I do not tarry over what Jerome thinks; let us rather inquire
what is true.   II, vii, 5

TRUTH, MISSING THE

But they [the philosophers] saw things in such a way that their
seeing did not direct them to the truth, much less enable them to
attain it! They are like a traveler passing through a field at night
who in a momentary lightning flash sees far and wide, but the sight
vanishes so swiftly that he is plunged again into the darkness of the
night before he can take even a step—let alone be directed on his
way by its help. Besides, although they may chance to sprinkle their
books with droplets of truth, how many monstrous lies defile them!
In short, they never even sensed that assurance of God's benevolence
toward us (without which man's understanding can only be filled
with boundless confusion). Human reason, therefore, neither approaches, nor strives toward, nor even takes a straight aim at, this
truth: to understand who the true God is or what sort of God he
wishes to be toward us.   II, ii, 18

TYRANNY

But however these deeds of men are judged in themselves, still the Lord accomplished his work through them alike when he broke the bloody scepters of arrogant kings and when he overturned intolerable governments. Let the princes hear and be afraid. But we must, in the meantime, be very careful not to despise or violate that authority of magistrates, full of venerable majesty, which God has established by the weightiest decrees, even though it may reside with the most unworthy men, who defile it as much as they can with their own wickedness. For, if the correction of unbridled despotism is the Lord's to avenge, let us not at once think that it is entrusted to us, to whom no command has been given except to obey and suffer.   IV, xx, 31

UNBELIEF

We ought not to seek any more intimate proof of this than that unbelief is, in all men, always mixed with faith.   III, ii, 4

The matter stands thus: Unbelief does not hold sway within believers' hearts, but assails them from without. It does not mortally wound them with its weapons, but merely harasses them, or at most so injures them that the wound is curable. Faith, then, as Paul teaches, serves as our shield.   III, ii, 21

VICE

The very vices that infest us we take pains to hide from others, while we flatter ourselves with the pretense that they are slight and insignificant, and even sometimes embrace them as virtues. . . . Hence arises such insolence that each one of us, as if exempt from the common lot, wishes to tower above the rest, and loftily and savagely abuses every mortal man, or at least looks down upon him as an inferior.   III, vii, 4

VIRTUE

For by the virtue contrary to the vice, men usually mean abstinence from that vice. We say that the virtue goes beyond this to contrary duties and deeds. Therefore in this commandment, "You shall not kill," men's common sense will see only that we must abstain from wronging anyone or desiring to do so. Besides this, it contains, I say, the requirement that we give our neighbor's life all the help we can. To prove that I am not speaking unreasonably: God forbids us to hurt or harm a brother unjustly, because he wills that the brother's life be dear and precious to us. So at the same time he requires those duties of love which can apply to its preservation. And thus we see how the purpose of the commandment always discloses to us whatever it there enjoins or forbids us to do.

II, viii, 9

VOCATION

Therefore each individual has his own kind of living assigned to him by the Lord as a sort of sentry post so that he may not heedlessly wander about throughout life . . . It is enough if we know that the Lord's calling is in everything the beginning and foundation of well-doing. And if there is anyone who will not direct himself to it, he will never hold to the straight path in his duties. For no one, impelled by his own rashness, will attempt more than his calling will permit, because he will know that it is not lawful to exceed its bounds. A man of obscure station will lead a private life ungrudgingly so as not to leave the rank in which he has been placed by God. Again, it will be no slight relief from cares, labors, troubles, and other burdens for a man to know that God is his guide in all these things. The magistrate will discharge his functions more willingly; the head of the household will confine himself to his duty; each man will bear and swallow the discomforts, vexations, weariness, and anxieties in his way of life, when he has been persuaded that the burden was laid upon him by God. From this will arise also a singular consolation: that no task will be so sordid and base, provided you obey your calling in it, that it will not shine and be reckoned very precious in God's sight.   III, x, 6

VOWS

Let our first precaution in vows, therefore, be never to proceed to any avowal without our conscience first making sure that it attempts nothing rash. But it shall be free of the danger of rashness when it has God going before it and dictating as from his own Word what is good or unprofitable to do.   IV, xiii, 2

WAR

But kings and people must sometimes take up arms to execute such public vengeance. On this basis we may judge wars lawful which are so undertaken. For if power has been given them to preserve the tranquility of their dominion, to restrain the seditious stirrings of restless men, to help those forcibly oppressed, to punish evil deeds—can they use it more opportunely than to check the fury of one who disturbs both the repose of private individuals and the common tranquility of all, who raises seditious tumults, and by whom violent oppressions and vile misdeeds are perpetrated? If they ought to be the guardians and defenders of the laws, they should also overthrow the efforts of all whose offenses corrupt the discipline of the laws. Indeed, if they rightly punish those robbers whose harmful acts have affected only a few, will they allow a whole country to be afflicted and devastated by robberies with impunity? For it makes no difference whether it be a king or the lowest of the common folk who invades a foreign country in which he has no right, and harries it as an enemy. All such must, equally, be considered as robbers and punished accordingly. Therefore, both natural equity and the nature of the office dictate that princes must be armed not only to restrain the misdeeds of private individuals by judicial punishment, but also to defend by war the dominions entrusted to their safekeeping, if at any time they are under enemy attack. And the Holy Spirit declares such wars to be lawful by many testimonies of Scripture.   IV, xx, 11

But if anyone object against me that in the New Testament there exists no testimony or example which teaches that war is a thing lawful for Christians, I answer first that the reason for waging war which existed of old still persists today; and that, on the other hand, there is no reason that bars magistrates from defending their subjects. Secondly, I say that an express declaration of this matter is not to be sought in the writings of the apostles; for their purpose is not to fashion a civil government, but to establish the spiritual

Kingdom of Christ. Finally, that it is there shown in passing that Christ by his coming has changed nothing in this respect. For if Christian doctrine (to use Augustine's words) condemned all wars, the soldiers asking counsel concerning salvation should rather have been advised to cast away their weapons and withdraw completely from military service. But they were told: "Strike no man, do no man wrong, be content with your wages." When he taught them to be content with their wages, he certainly did not forbid them to bear arms.   IV, xx, 12

WILL, GOD'S

But even though his [God's] will is one and simple in him, it appears manifold to us because, on account of our mental incapacity, we do not grasp how in divers ways it wills and does not will something to take place . . . so that in a wonderful and ineffable manner nothing is done without God's will, not even that which is against his will. For it would not be done if he did not permit it; yet he docs not unwillingly permit it, but willingly; nor would he, being good, allow evil to be done, unless being also almighty he could make good even out of evil."   I, xviii, 3

Here it is not a question of his secret will, by which he controls all things and directs them to their end. For even though Satan and men violently inveigh against him, he knows that by his incomprehensible plan he not only turns aside their attacks but so orders it that he may do through them what he has decreed.   III, xx, 43

For God's will is so much the highest rule of righteousness that whatever he wills, by the very fact that he wills it, must be considered righteous.   III, xxiii, 2

Albeit the solution we have elsewhere advanced is quite sufficient: although to our perception God's will is manifold, he does not will this and that in himself, but according to his diversely manifold wisdom, as Paul calls it, he strikes dumb our senses until it is given to us to recognize how wonderfully he wills what at the moment seems to be against his will.   III, xxiv, 17

WILL, MAN'S

Similarly the will, because it is inseparable from man's nature, did not perish, but was so bound to wicked desires that it cannot strive after the right.   II, ii, 12

For it always follows that nothing good can arise out of our will until it has been reformed; and after its reformation, in so far as it is good, it is so from God, not from ourselves.   II, iii, 8

Somewhere Augustine compares man's will to a horse awaiting its rider's command, and God and the devil to its riders. "If God sits astride it," he says, "then as a moderate and skilled rider, he guides it properly, spurs it if it is too slow, checks it if it is too swift, restrains it if it is too rough or too wild, subdues it if it balks, and leads it into the right path. But if the devil saddles it, he violently drives it far from the trail like a foolish and wanton rider, forces it into ditches, tumbles it over cliffs, and goads it into obstinacy and fierceness." Since a better comparison does not come to mind, we shall be satisfied with this one for the present.   II, iv, 1

WINE

Surely ivory and gold and riches are good creations of God, permitted, indeed appointed, for men's use by God's providence. And we have never been forbidden to laugh, or to be filled, or to join new possessions to old or ancestral ones, or to delight in musical harmony, or to drink wine. True indeed. But where there is plenty, to wallow in delights, to gorge oneself, to intoxicate mind and heart with present pleasures and be always panting after new ones—such are very far removed from a lawful use of God's gifts. Away, then, with uncontrolled desire, away with immoderate prodigality, away with vanity and arrogance—in order that men may with a clean conscience cleanly use God's gifts.   III, xix, 9

Now, it is clear what great superstition over vows plagued the the world for some centuries. One person vowed that he would be abstemious, as if abstinence from wine were of itself worship pleasing to God.   IV, xiii, 7

WISDOM, PARTS OF

Nearly all the wisdom we possess, that is to say, true and sound wisdom, consists of two parts: the knowledge of God and of ourselves.

I, i, 1

WISDOM, SCRIPTURE AND

For our wisdom ought to be nothing else than to embrace with humble teachableness, and at least without finding fault, whatever is taught in Sacred Scripture.   I, xviii, 4

WISDOM, SPIRITUAL

We must now analyze what human reason can discern with regard to God's kingdom and to spiritual insight. This spiritual insight consists chiefly in three things: (1) knowing God; (2) knowing his fatherly favor in our behalf, in which our salvation consists; (3) knowing how to frame our life according to the rule of his law.

II, ii, 18

WORKS, BLESSING FROM

Good works, then, are pleasing to God and are not unfruitful for their doers. But they receive by way of reward the most ample benefits of God, not because they so deserve but because God's kindness has of itself set this value on them.   III, xv, 3

WORKS, CHARACTER SEEN BY

But again, let us keep in mind that the fulfillment of the Lord's mercy does not depend upon believers' works but that he fulfills the promise of salvation for those who respond to his call with upright life, because in those who are directed to the good by his Spirit he recognizes the only genuine insignia of his children.

III, xvii, 6

WORKS, FAITH AND

For our opponents are chiefly deceived in thinking that James is defining the manner of justification when he is attempting only to shatter the evil confidence of those who vainly pretended faith as an excuse for their contempt of good works.   III, xvii, 12

WORKS, GRACE AND

From this it appears that the word "to work" is not opposed to grace but refers to endeavor. Accordingly, it does not follow that believers are themselves the authors of their own salvation, or that salvation stems from their own works. What then? Once they are, by knowledge of the gospel and illumination of the Holy Spirit, called into the fellowship of Christ, eternal life begins in them. Now that God has begun a good work in them, it must also be made perfect until the Day of the Lord Jesus. It is, however, made perfect when, resembling their Heavenly Father in righteousness and holiness, they prove themselves sons true to their nature.   III, xviii, 1

WORKS, INADEQUACY OF

To sum up, if we seek salvation in works, we must keep the commandments by which we are instructed unto perfect righteousness. But we must not stop here unless we wish to fail in mid-course, for none of us is capable of keeping the commandments. Therefore, since we are barred from law righteousness, we must betake ourselves to another help, that is, to faith in Christ.   III, xviii, 9

WORKS, PERFECTION OF

So says Augustine in one place: "The righteousness of the saints in this world consists more in the forgiveness of sins than in perfection of virtues."   III, xi, 22

WORKS, REWARD OF

Works enjoined by God have their reward because the Lawgiver himself accepts them as evidence of obedience. Therefore, such works do not derive value from their own worth or merit but because God so highly values our obedience to him. Here I am speaking of the perfection in works which is enjoined by God, but is not performed by men. For the works of the law which we do, have grace only from God's free kindness, because in them our obedience is weak and defective.   IV, x, 15

WORKS, RIGHTEOUSNESS OF

If anyone should wonder why the apostle, not content with nam·
ing works, uses such a qualification, there is a ready explanation.
Though works are highly esteemed, they have their value from God's
approval rather than from their own worth. For who would dare
recommend works righteousness to God unless God himself approved? Who would dare demand a reward due unless he promised
it? Therefore, it is from God's beneficence that they are considered
worthy both of the name of righteousness and of the reward thereof.
And so, for this one reason, works have value, because through them
man intends to show obedience to God.   III, xi, 20

WORKS, SALVATION AND

For justification is withdrawn from works, not that no good
works may be done, or that what is done may be denied to be good,
but that we may not rely upon them, glory in them, or ascribe salvation to them.   III, xvii, 1

WORSHIP

Therefore, it is worship of God alone that renders men higher
than the brutes, and through it alone they aspire to immortality.
I, iii, 3

It is therefore no wonder that the Holy Spirit rejects as base all
cults contrived through the will of men; for in the heavenly mysteries, opinion humanly conceived, even if it does not always give
birth to a great heap of errors, is nevertheless the mother of error.
I, v, 13

INDEX OF SUBJECTS

149